Memoir

of

"A Sloppy, Spineless, Creature"
Surviving My Family and the British Class System

By

Rose Dudley

rosedudley1941@gmail.com

Cover Design by Jennifer Givner, Acapella Book Cover Design
Formatting by Sharon Brownlie

DEDICATION

This memoir is dedicated to my wonderful family:—my husband, John, my children, Helen and Wyatt, Alison and Eric, and Nicola and Marcel, and our seven beautiful grandchildren: Amanda, Nicholas, Raine, Maliya, Anika, Sienna and Sacha.

"Who people are can be determined not by what happens to them but by how they deal with it."
Rosalind MacPhee—*Picasso's Woman*

PROLOGUE

Hiraeth [n.]:—a homesickness for a home to which you cannot return, a home which maybe never was, the nostalgia, the yearning, the grief for the lost places of your past.

The old bus station has changed almost beyond recognition, hardly surprising in sixty or more years, but as I shake off my backpack, lower myself down onto the cold, metal bench and cast a glance over to where the mass of red and white school buses once waited in a neat line, I become, once again, a fragile, tormented, spineless teen, a notion of ugliness and self-loathing attempting to make myself invisible to the world.

Memories fade, are clouded or vague until they cling to the being of the past. Now, they begin to spread over me like a sticky, dark substance, the stains of which can never fully be removed. On this journey, I need to rediscover those places that will trigger the shadowy reflections that lie deep within my soul.

I glance around at what has become an open, deserted, cheerless space, devoid of buses and people, surrounded by crumbling cement block walls from which dying weeds protrude. A few fading flowers, dotted around the base of the benches, competing helplessly with careless feet, add to a feeling of desolation.

In the old days, there had been a fully staffed information office, now replaced, in the pursuit of economy and efficiency, by a few scattered, glass-encased timetables that one needs an advanced degree to decipher.

My college education continues to fail me dismally in dealing with the challenges of daily existence. So often, I am rendered helpless by what is erroneously called progress; it has succeeded in turning me into a seemingly doddering, old fogey before my time.

The information has become blurred by years of grime. I had tried to remove it by rubbing it with my sleeve, but the dirt has seeped under the glass. From the information that I had been able to gather, a bus is due within the hour, so I have resigned myself to a long wait.

With little enthusiasm, I remove a book from my backpack—*Green Gone Wrong—Dispatches from the Front Lines of Eco-Capitalism.*

"A really fascinating book—you'll love it," John had said as, at the last minute, I had searched frantically for something suitable to read on the plane.

"A good cure for jet-lag induced insomnia," I laughed, being all too familiar with John's assessment of "really fascinating." Now, I pray it won't send me to sleep before my bus arrives.

There are patches of blue in the sky, puffy clouds like those painted on the memory of children, a welcome warmth from a pale sun. A sudden, brisk wind wraps itself around my bare legs, whisking up chocolate bar wrappers and newspapers—blowing them across the wide expanse. Garbage twirls out of the wire basket bins that have been placed optimistically beside each bench.

As I try to make myself comfortable, an older, shaggy-bearded man in a worn trilby hat and a brown suit that has seen better days, approaches, shuffling slowly, weighed down by two cloth bags of shopping. Every few yards, he stops to put them down in order to take a drag from a cigarette that dangles from his bottom lip. He drops on to the bench beside me, finishes the cigarette and grinds it into the gravel with the heel of his boot, coughing uncontrollably as he does so. I move uneasily on my seat. I wonder if he will be taking a bus in my direction and, selfishly, hope that he will not.

"Are you waiting for the Newport bus?" I venture, when there is a pause in the next fit of coughing.

"Oh, aye, you's 'opin for that 'un? S'posed to be 'ere in a few minutes, but you can't bank on anythin' these days."

I just nod, not really knowing quite how to add value

to the conversation. He speaks like all the locals—a broad Welsh accent combined with the coarse dialect of the border county. It was how I spoke until, in my so awfully posh educational establishment, it became unacceptable. It grates on my memory.

"Where's you from then love?" he asks.

"I live in Canada now," I respond, "but I am originally from this area. I grew up near Raglan and went to school here in Monmouth."

"Oh aye, Canada you says—bet things is a lot better over there; you did well to get the 'ell outa this damn country. Everythin's gone to the dogs over 'ere if you ask me."

"Well things do seem to have changed a lot," I agree, wondering if ever there was a time in history—some golden era—when the Welsh didn't actually believe that the country had gone to the dogs.

"Canada, you says," he continues, lighting up his next cigarette and throwing the still burning match onto the ground. "Wish to 'ell I'd got outa 'ere when I was young—there's nothin' for young 'uns round 'ere no more—never wus. They's all on the dole the minute they gets outa school. Mind you, they's all gotta 'ave their big fancy cars an' they's all gallivanting off to Spain an' even Florida now is the latest fashion, if you can believe it? Can't see what the attraction of Florida is, with all those damned Yankees, meself. Like I said, aye, the damn country's gone to the dogs."

In a world of such rapid change, this forgotten corner, in so many ways, remains firmly closed and bolted in the last century.

The gentleman seems to be quite happy with just my occasional nod in response, but I am relieved when a bus finally appears.

"That's the one you's wantin' love," my companion indicates, and I feel a wave of relief that he is going to Abergavenny—well, that's if he's lucky. Already, I find myself infected by his pessimistic outlook on life in general.

"Well, it's been nice meetin' you like," he says more cheerfully, waving a friendly goodbye. "'Ave a nice time with the family, I s'pose it's family you's over to see?"

I feel just a tiny grain of guilt over my impatience with his coarse chatter and my judgement of him because of it, as I step onto the bus.

"Do you stop at Cuckoos' Row?" I ask the driver.

"Only if you wants me to love, I can take you just anywhere you wants, just say the word," he replies with characteristic British humour.

Edging up the aisle in search of a seat that has not had the stuffing torn out of it or been smeared with chewing gum or other matter of a dubious nature, I feel choked by that oh so familiar blend of diesel fumes, stale fish and chips and the results of Saturday night's over-consumption at the local pub.

Two older, corpulent women, loaded down with heavy overcoats, oversized handbags, umbrellas and shopping bags struggle up the steps and fall into the two front seats across the aisle from each other, groaning with the effort. I am shocked, as I realize that they are my contemporaries. I look for signs of recognition; could I have known them as children?

I could initiate a conversation, ask them if they attended Monmouth schools, discover if we know people in common, but, today, I am veiled securely behind my piteous, teenage self, a clone of the past.

Their conversation revolves around topics so relished by the Welsh—illness, death, memorable funerals. I settle in a seat far at the back of the bus, but it's impossible not to hear every word of their conversation.

"'Ow's it goin' then Elsie, since the op'?"

"Oh!—fair to middlin'—mustn't grumble—could be worse."

"Did you 'ear about ol' Dai Thomas then?—'e's not long for this world, so they says."

"Aye, but 'e's 'ad a good innin's and if you ask me 'is missus will be better off without the ol' bugger."

"Ol' Rhys Davies is back in the 'ospital again then?"

"Aye, but where there's life there's 'ope, aye, where there's life there's 'ope."

"I s'pose you 'eard about ol' Grace Williams?—she buried 'er 'usband a good few weeks ago, now. He made a lovely corpse."

I have to hide a smile as I picture ol' Grace, shovel in hand, covering the remains of her dead husband.

The conversation turns to the weather—seemingly, the only other serious topic of conversation in Wales, and I lose the thread as I look out at the lush green countryside, the sign of another wet summer.

In contrast to the green, the copses of oak, beech and birch trees are radiant in pink, crimson, bronze and burnished gold, at their peak, giving their best before the leaves fall and die, replenishing the earth, fading into a new beginning.

The road ahead is so narrow that the scrape of branches is harsh against the bus as it passes hazel, beech and hawthorn hedgerows stippled with rose-hips and blanketed in old man's beard, a sight that brings back a memory of the church pews strewn with it for Harvest Thanksgiving.

I'm thrown around in my seat as we hurtle past fields of grazing sheep stretching up the hillsides and black and white cows lumbering stately in line towards farm buildings. I wonder at nature's clock never failing to remind them that it will soon be milking time.

Fields of stubble proclaim harvest is over for another year. Some are already ploughed—neat red furrows, straight as arrows, soon to be worked and replanted with next season's crops.

Apples, plums, damsons and pears have been

picked, but remnants of bruised, overripe fruit lie decaying on the ground. I'm taken back to Bradley's orchard, drunk on the sickening sweet smell of rotting cider apples.

A translucent mist rises over the River Trothy as we bump over the bridge and I recall the daily thrill as we urged the driver to go faster and faster to hurl us out of our seats.

Cottage gardens are past their spring and summer prime but still a blaze of glory with rows of dahlias so cheerful in colours that only harmonize in nature, profusions of purple Michaelmas daisies and the last of the summer roses faithfully radiating joy until the first frost. I see my mother lovingly tending her rose garden so long gone.

The bus rattles along the old road, through Mitchel Troy where Hazel and I spent weekends with her grandmother, enjoying freedom from home restraints, past the Trothy Hotel where she married far too young and on to Dingestow where my mother's one remaining sister lives, her memory of the distant past still crystal clear, memory soon to be captured or lost in time.

As we approach my stop, the driver shouts,

"Cuckoos' Row!—Aye, looks like they's all flown today love," and he laughs, enjoying his own joke. "Where's you goin' from 'ere then love?" he asks as I alight, backpack slung over one shoulder.

"I'm walking up to Tregare—to Oakdale where I used to live—it's about three miles from here."

"Good God mun!" he shrieks in disbelief, as if I had just announced I was about to climb Everest. The two women in the front look equally bewildered. I know I have provided them with a more interesting topic of conversation for the remainder of their journey.

As the bus rattles on towards Newport, I stand silently, for a moment, at the beginning of the narrow lane in a spot which is so familiar that I might have been here yesterday. I pause, trying to picture my mother arriving at this very place over 70 years ago, lugging a cranky, crying infant, and setting off to walk the same route that I am about to follow to the home from which she had escaped but from which she could never stay away.

MEMOIR OF "A SLOPPY, SPINELESS, CREATURE"

CHAPTER ONE

"We are our stories. We tell them to stay alive or keep alive those who only live now in the telling."
Niall Williams—*History of the Rain*

Had my parents waited just two more months, I could have attended their wedding. As it was, my impending arrival may well have caused the eyes of the Roman Catholic priest to bulge right out of his head, on observing such a wilful affront to chastity. On the other hand, it was war time when blind eyes were being turned to all kinds of profligacy, so perhaps he could take it completely in his stride.

Not that the wedding would have been much cause for celebration. It took place at the austere Church of St. Xavier in what was then the wartime grey, cheerless town of Usk, Monmouthshire, South Wales, and the only other family member present was my aunt Blodwen, my mother's eldest sister—self-elected head of the family— the educated one who was always called upon for such occasions whether celebratory or vexing, the latter being infinitely more common.

My grandmother was from the "If you have not witnessed it, then it hasn't happened," school of thought, so she would have refused to attend the ceremony and forbidden my grandfather or any of her other children to be present. After all, it would have appeared that they were giving the marriage their seal of approval— accomplices in immorality.

"Whatever would the neighbours say?"

But, of course, the neighbours would have had lots to say, as they do in small rural communities where nothing of any real significance, other than a few tragic accidents involving farm machinery, might happen for years on end. They would have been delighted to feast on the juicy morsel of my mother's sin for a lifetime.

My mother, Irene, was nineteen years old on her wedding day—just a girl really. She came from a lengthy line of Joneses which is not difficult in a country where there are tens of thousands of them. Around thirteen percent of the population are Joneses—one of the more famous being Tom.

Most people are not aware that Tom wasn't a real Jones. He was born Tom Woodward and changed his name to his mother's maiden name. When he sings with such sentiment of "The Green, Green Grass of Home" one must agree that it sounds more heartfelt sung by a Jones rather than a Woodward.

The Joneses are intensely proud of their name. In November of 2006, they decided to bring together all the Joneses they could muster into the Millennium Centre in Cardiff, to outdo the Norbergs of Sweden—Norberg being the most common name in Sweden—who were trying to get themselves registered in *The Guinness Book of Records* for the most people of that name gathered in one place at the same time. Of course, the Joneses won hands down.

My mother's father, Philip Jones from Aberdare, had married her mother, born Sarah Jones, from Llangattock Lingoed, and they had rented a small farm or smallholding in rural South Wales. Aberdare and Llangattock Lingoed are only a stone's throw apart as the crow flies but would have been a great distance without transportation in the early nineteen hundreds, so it is a mystery how my grandparents managed to meet, conceive Aunt Blodwen and marry, in that order.

My father, Patrick Benjamin Lynch, who was to play a very small part in my life, was the black sheep of a large, Irish Catholic, farming family from Donegal. Over the years, his family would produce 33 of my first cousins, none of whom I would ever have the pleasure of knowing as I grew up. One of them still runs my Irish grandparents' farm in Buncrana, Co. Donegal.

Another mystery is why my father, along with tens of thousands of other Irish men, would deign to come over to Britain to support the war effort when the English had been beating the living daylights out of the Irish for centuries.

Soon after the marriage, my parents moved to Oxford where my father, a gunner in the Royal Artillery, was stationed. Prior to that, he had been stationed near my mother's home at Cuckoos' Row which is, presumably, how she met him. Would that not have given most sane people cause for hesitation? Clearly my mother saw no irony.

WWII was raging across Europe when I was born on the ninth of September 1941. This was only 38 years after the Wright Brothers had made their first successful flight, and only 22 years after a plane first made it all the way across the Atlantic. Three months after my birth, the Japanese bombed Pearl Harbour bringing America into the war.

The Nazis had already begun the massacre of Jews in Lithuania, and by 1945, they would have exterminated an estimated six million throughout Europe along with millions of gypsies, homosexuals, Jehovah's Witnesses and people with disabilities. Meanwhile, the world would ignore the appalling atrocities and learn absolutely nothing from them. There is so much luck in where one is born and into what faith.

I was born at John Ruskin College of Art, in Oxford in the county of Oxfordshire, England. My mother was not a Fine Arts student who suddenly went into labour, no matter how much I wish I could tell you that it had been so. Social status after all was, and still is, of supreme importance in Great Britain as I, growing up, would learn the hard way.

John Ruskin College was established by the eponymous benefactor in 1899 to provide education for the working-class and had been turned into a maternity hospital during the war.

I don't know how he would have reacted to the college being filled with bawling infants between 1941 and 1946, but since he was a prominent social thinker and his work emphasized the relationship between nature, art and society, I think he would have understood the connection and been tickled pink.

I feel rather proud of my association with such a prestigious gentleman. After all, it was Ruskin's work, *Unto This Last*, which dealt with inequality in society, that aroused Mahatma Gandhi's interest. Gandhi had made a point of visiting the college because he was so inspired by the work and generosity of John Ruskin, but that was ten years before my time—my first missed opportunity.

Ruskin's ideas are now widely recognized as having anticipated interest in environmentalism and sustainability, but for me to claim that my involvement in such issues in my old age could be the direct result of where I was born might be a bit of a stretch.

Immediately following my birth, I was baptized at a Roman Catholic church in Henley-on-Thames. The choice of that town, many miles from Oxford, will remain another mystery. Could it have been the capricious hand of fate? No one could have known, at the time, that Henley-on-Thames was to feature prominently in my future life.

Surrounded by 11 of my Irish cousins. My father's surviving sister, Aunt Mary, sits to my right.

I was named Rosemary Ann after my Irish grandmother, Rose Ann, with whom I would never have any contact, and of whom I would know nothing for 60 years until I finally went to Ireland to look up my large Irish family and visit my grandparents' grave in Buncrana churchyard.

I have always felt a little cheated that I had been born in England of an Irish father called Lynch because, just like Tom Jones who didn't want to be saddled with the very English sounding Woodward name, it has always been important for me to think of myself as Welsh and identify myself as such. Still, they say that when the cat had kittens in the oven, she didn't call them biscuits, so I feel somewhat vindicated.

When I was no more than a toddler, my mother moved back to the family home in Wales. Possibly, she had already deduced that my father was anything but a good catch, but it is more likely that while bombs were dropping on London, she may have felt that Oxford was in the danger zone. Rumours abound that Germany had made a pact with England that it would not bomb Oxford or Cambridge in exchange for England sparing German university towns, but those rumours have never been substantiated.

That she would return, so soon, to a home from which she had escaped, I would come to understand in the course of time. While we strive so earnestly to free ourselves from painful memories, we become so hopelessly entangled in our roots.

The move, if nothing else, bestowed upon me a childhood set in the beauty and solitude of rural Wales for which I would be forever grateful.

My grandparents were eking out a frugal existence in a tiny community on an old coaching road—along which mail coaches or stagecoaches used to run—halfway between Monmouth and Abergavenny. Two of the original mail coach stops that have been converted into basic residential properties still exist.

Tregare—or Tregaer in Welsh—where I would spend my childhood, was nothing more than a collection of farms and farm cottages and, other than a church and a school, had nothing even to qualify it as a village. There had been a pub there in the past, but it is hard to imagine how it could ever have generated enough custom in a neighbourhood where having a sherry on Christmas Day was considered a very bold move indeed.

My great grandmother, also Sarah Jones, was living in the former pub at the time, along with my great aunt Bessie Jones whose actual relationship to us was never disclosed, and who, according to my grandmother, was "not right in the head." My grandmother accused large numbers of people of not being "right in the head," but she could have been correct about my aunt Bessie as I have vivid memories of her behaving in ways that could hardly be considered normal even in a place like Tregare.

She was fascinated by a pair of my crude, homemade stilts and became surprisingly proficient at walking on them. Aunt Bessie, thin as a stick, lurching across the fields on stilts, attracted rather more attention from passers-by than anyone had bargained for and caused much embarrassment to my grandmother who would have preferred poor Bessie to be banished to "the looney bin."

Tregare was three miles from the nearest public transportation. There was no electricity, telephone or running water and quite possibly several residents who didn't even know that such things had been invented. Many of them, in the whole of their lives, would travel no further than Monmouth or Abergavenny.

The journey from Oxford is only 80 miles, but it would have been a harrowing, long day for my mother, obliged to use a succession of trains and buses, followed by that long walk from Cuckoos' Row to her home carrying a baby along with all her worldly goods. She would have been so relieved to reach the peace and tranquillity of the countryside.

It was springtime when she brought me home, a time when the narrow country lanes are brimming with sweet scented flowers—primroses, cowslips, violets—blooming hedgerows alive with the songs of blackbirds and thrushes—air fragrant with the scent of newly cut grass and the fields resonant with the sounds of new-born lambs bleating to the throaty calls of their anxious mothers—a delight to the senses.

We would have passed little stone cottages built right up to the edge of what only a few years earlier had been a single track, and landmarks that would become very familiar to me over the next eighteen years, Marble Hall, Waterloo, Park Lane—places that could only have been named by a person either with an illusion of grandeur or an exceedingly warped sense of humour. We also would have passed by the only red telephone box for miles—our link to the outside world, other than the postman, and the solid stone school, built in 1875, which my mother and her siblings had attended and where I would embark on my education in three more years or so.

Our destination was "Oakdale," built in 1909, where my grandparents had lived since soon after their marriage. It had originally been built by the landowners as a shooting lodge and had a small bungalow attached, presumably for guests who came for the pheasant and rabbit shoot. For this reason, my family had always been referred to as "Joneses, the Shooting Box."

Oakdale—The Shooting Box

This title, of course, helped to distinguish our family from all the other Joneses in the neighbourhood. Even the next-door neighbours were Joneses—known simply as Mr. and Mrs. Jones. No one ever referred to their neighbours by their Christian names, even though they might have lived next door to them for 50 years or more. When I say neighbours, incidentally, the next-door Joneses lived about half a mile on down the lane.

Before the Jones family became our neighbours, the Johnsons had lived in that house. I do not remember them, but I feel as if I knew Mrs. Johnson quite well. I was told so many times how,

"Ol' Mrs. Johnson was as wide as she was tall, 'er dresses were old curtains wrapped around 'er bulk, it 'ad been one 'ell of a job to lay 'er out, and it took a special, extra-large coffin to accommodate 'er vast remains."

The other frequently repeated, interesting information I acquired about the Johnson family was that "they didn't have a pot to piss in."

Our other close neighbours were the Bradleys who lived about half a mile across the fields. No other house was visible from our house.

From the exterior, Oakdale was imposing, compared to the other little stone and whitewashed cottages and farm houses in the area. One might have believed that the Jones family was a cut above the neighbours, but one would have been barking up the wrong tree.

As she rounded the last corner, my mother would have seen the Black Mountains—the peak of the Sugar Loaf and the Blorenge behind which, on summer evenings, the sun set in ribbons of exquisite colour. And then the house—a lonely, stark looking sentinel standing against an extensive backdrop of tall trees collectively known as the Park Wood—a big, square, red brick and yellow stucco structure topped by a grey, slate-tiled roof and surrounded by a black, wrought iron fence set upon rounded, low brick walls.

During my teens, Park Wood, which had been my childhood playground, would be taken over by the Forestry Commission. All the deciduous trees would be removed and replaced with fir trees. As they grew, they would block the afternoon sun, creating a darker backdrop to Oakdale and giving it an even more ominous appearance.

To the east side stood a large wooden building called the motor-house, a somewhat erroneous label as it would be many years before anyone owned a motor of any kind. It was mainly used as storage for hay and other animal feed.

Close to the house, but at a respectable distance, was the stone, whitewashed coal house and the outhouse—the W.C—matching the red brick of the house. In earlier days, some resourceful person had planted lilac and orange blossom trees which blocked the view of the W.C. from the lane as well as the pungent smell, at least during the blooming season.

Across the road from the house were the farm fields, poultry coops and a cow shed in front of which stood an ever-increasing pile of cow dung which provided fertilizer for the garden.

Most of the garden was turned over to vegetables, but flowers were also grown to be sold at Abergavenny market, providing a meagre supplement to my grandparents' income.

As my mother arrived at Oakdale that day, exhausted after her long journey, I know she would have been filled with such apprehension. She would have been anticipating the welcome that awaited her:

"I told you so, running off with that rotter, Pat. No good ever comes of 'is sort."

So often, I have been told,

"You screamed like a banshee all the way home."

Could I have had a premonition about my future life? I was about to meet my grandmother.

CHAPTER TWO

"Some family trees have beautiful leaves, and some have just a bunch of nuts. Remember, it is the nuts that make the tree worth shaking."
Author Unknown.

When one thinks of grandmothers, one thinks warm and fuzzy. By a long shot, that does not describe mine. The dictionary definition of warm and fuzzy states, "any person or thing that gives others comfort, reassurance or a friendly feeling." My grandmother was the very antithesis. In fact, if Robert Louis Stevenson's book had not been published in 1886, two years prior to my grandmother's birth, we might have believed that he had used her as the inspiration for *The Strange Case of Dr. Jekyll and Mr. Hyde.*

Her face to the straitened world in which we lived was the epitome of sweetness and light, but behind those brick and stucco walls, Mr. Hyde raged with a violent force. Being raised in that household was akin to living in the shadow of an active volcano. Short periods of calm would be interspersed with a build-up of anger that would erupt in a mighty explosion spewing forth venom and striking out at everyone in the line of fire, sending them scuttling like rats to their holes.

Even in a neighbourhood of eccentrics—the country characters one sees in British dramas—she stood out like a Belisha beacon. A woman of diminutive height but ample girth, she strode around the farm, often pursued by a collection of ducks, chickens and turkeys swarming around her ankles, wearing her Wellington boots, and a wraparound, print apron to protect clothes that never ever saw the light of day. With her sleeves rolled up to the elbows, she meant business.

At times, she would suddenly stop in her tracks and begin to mutter incoherent words under her breath.

That behaviour usually heralded the onset of one of her black moods and we knew, instinctively, that it was wise for the rats to make themselves scarce.

In earlier photographs, my grandmother is seen with poker-straight, grey hair, but my first vivid memories of her coincide with the coming of the revolutionary Tony Home Permanent. Forever after that questionable contribution to fashion appeared, her tightly permed hair was always wound up in metal curlers as if in preparation for a later special event. Having worn the curlers all day, she would remove them at night, proclaiming them to be too uncomfortable to sleep in, brush her hair and go to bed.

Only one event could disrupt that routine—a thunderstorm. At the first rumble, she would be stricken with fear, and those curlers would be out in a trice and hidden under the tablecloth along with the cutlery and every other metal object in sight. Having covered all the mirrors and opened all the doors to provide an escape route for "any wayward thunderbolt that might drop down the chimney," she would drag all family members present under the stairs to wait out the storm. There we would crouch together, in the darkness, crushed amongst disused family trappings, hands over our ears in a desperate attempt to shut out the terrifying claps of thunder shaking the house and my grandmother's beseeching prayers to God to deliver us from the jaws of death.

The trademark Wellington boots were worn winter and summer—in the winter to slog through the mud and cow dung—in the summer to "keep out the adders." To solve the problem of overheating, my grandmother always cut holes in the toes of the boots to let in the air.

Only once had she ever encountered an adder around the farm, but I was constantly reminded that one of the neighbourhood girls had been bitten by one while picking primroses which was possibly the reason why I soon developed an irrational fear of snakes to add to my fear of thunderstorms.

She kept her teeth in a jar behind the sewing machine on the sideboard and wore them only for special occasions—whist drives or social evenings in the church hall which she attended bearing an uncanny resemblance to the Cheshire Cat in *Alice in Wonderland.* They were so ill-fitting that she could not eat while wearing them in case they fell out so, like the person who can't wait to throw off uncomfortable shoes, she could not wait to get home to return them to the jar behind the sewing machine which she did with a huge sigh of relief before tucking into huge hunks of bread and cheese with her rock-hard gums. Living without teeth never caused her a moment's indigestion despite what today's medical experts might tell you about the importance of chewing your food.

Her pale skin and Roman nose gave her a rather witch-like appearance. She wore no makeup or adornments of any kind—"only those ol' Germans and gypsies abased themselves in such ways." Her encounters with Germans were, as far as I know, about as frequent as her encounters with adders, but that did not prevent her from being an authority on the subject.

My grandparents had seven children, six of whom survived, a good percentage for those times before the invention of penicillin by Alexander Fleming in 1928.

Four children at the Tregare School—Blodwen, Philip, Irene, (centre) and Phyllis

Blodwen, the eldest, has already made a cameo appearance. She was named after my great aunt Blodwen Jones, as if one relative by that name wasn't enough in the family.

She was, to say it politely, on the heavy side which she falsely attributed to a glandular problem. She had dark, tightly permed hair—another Tony Home Perm convert—wore very thick glasses which she had a habit of pushing up to the top of her nose to read the newspaper, and she tottered around on very high heeled shoes from which her chubby feet bulged like balloons under pressure—a barrel on legs—a character from a Beryl Cook painting.

She did her nurse's training in Hereford and spent her life caring for the mentally ill which apparently afforded her no special skill in dealing with her own mother's mental instability but contributed to her eventually becoming more like one of the inmates herself.

She adopted an artificial air of upward mobility, puffing out her chest like a turkey attracting a mate, looking down upon her less educated siblings and proudly voting Conservative.

Because of her attitude, she was often the butt of family jokes, but, in truth, she was kind and generous. If it had not been for her, I would never have enjoyed a holiday.

When I was seven or eight years old, she took my cousin and me to London, and for several summers she took us to seaside resorts. Compared to the rest of the neighbourhood children, we were world travellers. Our contemporaries had to be satisfied with the annual Sunday School outing to Barry Island. We had fed the pigeons in Trafalgar Square, we had been to Blackpool and seen Reginald Dickson, in person, performing on his organ in the tower. We had been to Bournemouth, Weston-Super-Mare and Weymouth and seen shows featuring comedians who most people had only heard on the radio. It could have given us such a feeling of superiority over our friends.

Aunt Blodwen, as it turned out, did have an ulterior motive, but we didn't hold it against her that she was merely using us as decoys. Unknown to my grandmother, she had always made prior arrangements to meet a boyfriend in her chosen seaside town. We were never actually introduced to her mystery men, neither did she speak of them, but often, without explanation, she would quietly tell us that she "had things to do," hand us a bag-full of pennies to play the slot machines in the arcades and disappear for an afternoon or an evening. That was our idea of heaven—a whole afternoon spent in the faint hope of winning the jackpot until every penny had disappeared.

We always teased Aunt Blodwen that we knew exactly what she was up to,

On the first of several of Aunt Blodwen's sexual trysts—Trafalgar Square in London

although we could never have imagined, in our innocence, that someone of her age and extensive girth could be engaging in illicit sex. We threatened that we would tell our grandmother what she was up to but we knew, only too well, that information such as that had to be kept from her at all costs and, besides, we were smart enough to know that it would have put an abrupt end to any future holidays.

Phyllis came next in line but not in importance. She

was the first, in the eyes of her mother, to bring disgrace to the family by becoming pregnant by a neighbouring farmer in her late teens. I discovered, years later, that there was a court case over that scandal in which my grandmother tried to prove that it was a case of rape, but a neighbour, Walter Bradley, who for ever after would remain a pariah in the eyes of my grandmother, apparently gave evidence to the contrary, so the case was dropped.

To avoid gossip, a common solution in those days was to send the pregnant girl away and that is exactly what one would have expected a woman like my grandmother to have done, but recently, I learned that she chose to keep Phyllis hidden at home away from prying eyes. I can only begin to imagine the recriminations she would have suffered and the guilt which she would have lived through during those long months.

Another of Aunt Blodwen's clandestine meetings with a mystery man—in Backpool

Phyllis was kindness itself—gentle and giving. She was comfortably plump—her body as soft as a favourite old cushion. Her fine, straight hair was silky to the touch and her cheeks round and rosy like ripened apples. After her perceived sin, she spent the rest of her life trying so hard to make amends.

Her son, Haydn, my cousin, was brought up by our grandmother who constantly reminded him what a burden he was, frequently threatened to send him back to his real father and told him that if it had not been for her magnanimity he would have ended up in the Workhouse. Kindness and tact were not exactly my grandmother's strengths.

Haydn was four years older than me and like a big brother. He was a willowy, delicate looking boy with wispy blond hair and a pale complexion, but his waif-like appearance belied his considerable strength. As we grew up, we formed an unbreakable bond, cemented by the bizarre treatment at the hands of our crazy grandmother.

Philip was the only living son. He and Blodwen both had the benefit of a grammar school education paid for, in part, by the sacrifice of the others who were forced to leave school at the age of fourteen to take up menial jobs to support the family.

He was tall and dark and, according to rumour, quite a hit with the women, many of whom he led on for years with no honourable intent. During the war, he made the grave mistake of falling in love with a German girl. The fallout from that was worse than the Blitz so, understandably, he became extremely secretive about his life afterwards and no one in the family ever really knew what he did for a living or bothered to ask.

He would often turn up, unannounced, on weekends to work on the farm, and occasionally, a distraught, pretty girl would come in search of him. He would tell his sisters to lie about his whereabouts and refuse to see her.

On one occasion, when I was old enough, it fell to me to deliver the unwelcome news to one—Kitty Pearl, a young attractive blond. I felt uncomfortable about lying to her, and worse, because I understood that she knew I was lying. She turned away in tears before walking the three miles back to Cuckoos' Row. Philip did not appear to show the slightest bit of sympathy or embarrassment about the effort that she had gone to in order to seek him out. Eventually, I would come to have a better understanding of his reasons for hiding away.

In his fifties, he married a lovely, cultured woman, Diana, whom he courted long enough to ensure that she was past her childbearing years but young enough to care for him in his advancing age. Now, as he approaches 98, it appears that his ruse is paying dividends.

Only recently, I learned that he had been previously married and has a son, Robin Jones, yet one more cousin who I would never have the pleasure of knowing. Who knows how many more there were? Most families have a skeleton or two in their closet. Our closet was already exploding at the hinges.

Uncle Philip's philandering ways, however, were of no consequence to Haydn and me. We loved his visits; he was great fun. No sooner was he in the house, Haydn and I would be clambering all over him, clinging to his knees and begging him to throw us into the air. He was the father figure that neither of us would ever know.

My mother, Irene, was followed quickly by Marion and then Maisie. Soon after their births, my grandmother kicked my grandfather out of the marital bed—a harsh form of birth control, but the only one she knew. She then occupied the large front bedroom, my grandfather the smaller back one and everyone else, sometimes as many as six, slept together in the remaining one.

Maisie was a nymph-like, dark-haired, poor-sighted version of her oldest sister. She was exempt from supporting her older brother and sisters due to a "weak chest." She was kept at home and, in the rare calm periods, enjoyed a fair amount of mollycoddling.

She learned to play the piano rather well and eventually became the church organist, though that was by no means her greatest talent. She had an extraordinary ability to faint at opportune times which averted more than one family crisis and could easily have won her a coveted place at the Royal Academy of Dramatic Art.

Having lived the easy life of an invalid, she surprised everyone by leaving home in her twenties to accept a job as a bus conductress, the rigours of which, one surely would have thought, were hardly suitable for one with a "weak chest." Maisie certainly knew how to play her cards. She lived to a ripe old age, becoming a wealthy property owner in the process.

Irene, my mother, was also a wisp of a girl—very attractive with a good figure. Despite limited funds, she was always fashionably dressed, like her sister Maisie. Her light brown hair was worn according to the fashion of the day. She couldn't pass a mirror without smiling approvingly at what she saw.

My mother aged 25 in 1946. She was very much aware of her appeal.

Marion was the prettiest one in the family, having inherited the olive skin and dark hair of her father. She had an exceptional singing voice and possibly could have been an opera star had she been born into the right family, but she did not have the confidence, or the encouragement from her parents so, mostly, she sang at social evenings in the local towns and the village hall.

I thought she had the voice of an angel. From an early age, I was transfixed by her voice, and I memorized the words of the songs that she sang. My favourite was:

"Bless this house, oh Lord we pray,
Make it safe by night and day.
Bless these walls so firm and stout
Keeping want and trouble out.

Bless the roof and chimneys tall,
Let thy peace lie over all.
Bless this door that it may prove
Ever open to joy and love."

Looking back, I think that might have been her own personal prayer. Perhaps, as time went on, it became mine too.

Phyllis and Irene were never given the benefit of any education, musical or otherwise, but they both had special interests that gave them such pleasure. Without need for words, they would pass on those interests to Haydn and me—pleasures that would be sustained throughout our lives.

Phyllis loved books, especially poetry. She owned a battered old copy of the poetry of Walter de La Mare. It always fell open to the same page—to the poem, "Nod" which was the one that I insisted she read to me repeatedly. Those words are as musical to me now as they were then:

"Softly along the road of evening
In a twilight dim with rose,
Wrinkled with age and drenched with dew,
Old Nod, the shepherd, goes."

My mother, I would discover, took an almost spiritual delight in the sensuality of nature—its sounds and scents—its beauty and moods in the changing seasons. It was through her acute observations that I learned the names of all the birds, and the wild flowers and plants that grew in profusion around us.

Four sisters—left to right—Phyllis, Blodwen, Marion, Irene. Missing—Maisie

My grandfather was a slight, quiet, unassuming, pale shadow of a man who yearned for nothing more than a peaceful life, something there was clearly no hope of him ever attaining in this one. He hurried about with his head down in an effort to make himself as invisible as possible.

He wore an old trilby hat over his scant, wispy hair, and an even older brown suit, the trousers of which was tied around the ankles with binder-twine to keep the legs from dragging in the mud. It was rare to see him without a cigarette or a piece of straw sticking out of his mouth, and he had a habit of standing and staring across the fields to the distant hills. Years later, when I became familiar with the words of W.H. Davis's poem—"Leisure."

> "What is this life if full of care
> We have no time to stand and stare?
> No time to stand beneath the boughs
> And stare as long as sheep or cows?"

I always wanted to believe that the poem had been written about my grandfather.

My grandparents with Aunt Blodwen and Aunt Marion

Like almost everyone we knew in those days, he smoked Woodbines—the cigarettes of the working-class. Upper-class types chose cigarettes that they felt were more sophisticated, like Regals and Du Maurier's—they had filters which to them smacked of refinement. Eventually, Woodbines would have filters too, but by that time, they would forever be associated with the lower classes. No self-respecting snob would be caught smoking them.

How times change! Nowadays, no self-respecting person would be caught smoking, a hazardous journey through snobbery to the grave. It reminds one of the story of coarse unrefined bread, once the food of the poor, shunned by the upper-classes in preference for refined white bread. Offer white bread to the discerning orthorexics of today, and they'll make you feel that you are poisoning them.

On a battered old bicycle, my grandfather pedalled off every day to work at the Jenkins's farm—Wern-y-Melyn. His own smallholding could not generate enough income to support his large family.

Tired and worn, he would return late in the evening to do the work on his own farm. In the winter, it was often bitterly cold and dark by the time he had brought in the cows for milking, tended to the sheep or retrieved wayward animals that had broken out into other farmers' fields during the day. He would leave the house after a meagre supper of cold meat and potatoes or bacon and eggs, carrying a rusty old hurricane lamp to light his way.

I always watched to see when his chores had been completed. As soon as I saw the warm, comforting glow of that light bobbing down the fields towards the house, I knew that he would soon be safe and warm inside.

Every Sunday, he would wash his sunburned hands and face and sometimes soak his feet in a bowl of water in front of the fire. I don't remember him ever taking a bath. Then he would don his best but somewhat crumpled brown suit, attach his bicycle clips, pump up the tires and ride his rickety old machine to church.

He went not out of any strong religious belief, but because his wife made his life a living hell if he even dared to suggest that he just felt too tired. She rarely went herself, but she demanded that the family should always be represented, especially as my grandfather was one of the churchwardens:

"'ow will it look if the bloody churchwarden isn't there?—what will people say?"

Often, he would be the only person in the congregation other than the vicar's wife, but he knew only too well that it would have been ill-advised to point that out.

How vividly I can describe my family's exterior guise, but how little I would ever know about their inner feelings. Like buds on my mother's rose bushes, nipped by a late frost and failing to open with the warmth of June, their emotions were locked forever under too many impenetrable layers.

This was the family that I had inherited. These were the people to whom I had come home—the people who would shape my life.

CHAPTER THREE

"Your memories from your early childhood seem to have such purchase on your emotions; they are so concrete."
Dana Spiotta

For the first few years of my life, my mother and I, and my father—when he wasn't drinking himself under the table in a local pub, or lying face up in the gutter, bruised and battered from a fight and failing to show up for days—lived in the bungalow beside the main house away from the wrath of my grandmother.

The house had been occupied by Mr. and Mrs. Robinson prior to our arrival. "Ol' Robinson" suffered from shell shock acquired in WWI which apparently gave his face a constant look of terror. He was also handicapped, but whether that was because of a war injury was not clear. He had occupied a bed in the kitchen for years until he finally succumbed.

After his demise, several people, my grandmother included, reported seeing him running through the woods behind the house, staggering across the fields or sitting on the roof, relaxing in the moonlight. Clearly, he became more agile in death than he had been in life and was obviously enjoying his new-found freedom, after having been confined to his kitchen bed for so long.

For years after he passed on, any strange noise was put down to a visit from Mr. Robinson. He might even have been our most frequent visitor. When the back gate mysteriously clanged at night or crunching footsteps were heard on the gravel outside, my grandmother would declare in a matter of fact way,

"There's Ol' Robinson up to 'is tricks again."

My memories in those early years are few and the sequence uncertain. It is fascinating to ponder why certain incidences stick out so vividly in my mind while others are buried so deeply and forever. It is also amazing how I can hold in remembrance all the senses that were evoked in childhood; the scent of freshly mown grass, lilac, orange blossom, bluebells, primroses, and the effect of rain after a dry spell transport me immediately back to childhood. As the first snowdrops poke through the frozen earth in my garden, I see them suspended modestly on delicate stems, appearing every year, on cue, beside our orchard gate, and with the touch of bracken, I can still conjure up the tingling sensation that I felt as it brushed against my bare legs on my way to the well for water.

One of my earliest recollections is the Peace Day celebrations at the end of WWII when I would have been about four years old. This would have been such a memorable day for everyone signalling the end of a six-year war, but it was not the actual celebration and the joy of world peace that I recall. Peace was insignificant to my immediate needs.

Due to a thunderstorm, I was not permitted to stay to see the fireworks. Instead, I was dragged home along Park Lane protesting loudly; that was possibly the second time that I screamed like a banshee. There were no stairs to hide under in our part of the house, so most of the evening, I cried pathetically at the window while the storm raged outside, flashes of lightning lit up the sky, deafening claps of thunder shook the very foundations of the house and the rain beat horizontally against the window.

I remember, so vividly, trying with my finger to race the drops that ran down the outside of the pane and playing in the puddle of tears that I had made on the window sill inside. Sometimes, so caught up in the game, I would forget to cry for a moment and then remember why I was crying and bawl loudly again to try to make my mother feel guilty enough to change her mind. I failed.

Today, a crack of thunder or the sound of fireworks can immediately take me back to that early experience.

Perhaps it is why I have a dislike and a mild fear of both, although being dragged under the stairs by a terrified, praying grandmother during countless thunderstorms undoubtedly contributes to that fear.

A person who became very important to me in my young life, possibly prior to this incident, was Anne Driver who came to me, every week, through the auspices of the B.B.C. Home Service. Her voice still reverberates in my head. She introduced a weekly programme for schools called Music and Movement for Infants. I waited in anticipation every week.

In infants' schools, all around Britain, children were required to strip down to their underwear and leap about to the music and voice of Anne Driver. The removal of their clothes probably traumatized many of them. Currently, the practice would probably result in teachers being accused of sexual abuse. Meanwhile, at home, I was in my element leaping in and out of the chairs and around the dining room table with not a stitch on.

The only reference to my father that I remember was being told to get my clothes back on before he came home. It's odd to think that Anne Driver is more memorable to me than my own father. While I can still remember the songs that she played—Cherry Ripe and Golden Slumbers, to name two—sadly, I cannot put a face to my father as a young man or remember one thing about him.

Often, events which we think we remember are ones that have been talked about so frequently that we think of them as memories. One such event, the details of which had a profound and lasting effect on me, was the day that the postman arrived at the house bearing a telegram. Throughout the war years, every mother, wife and sweetheart knew what that meant. It was what they all dreaded for six long years—those heartbreaking words—It is my painful duty to inform you.......

My Uncle Philip was a soldier serving in France at

the time, so my grandmother automatically panicked believing that the postman was bearing news of her son's death. It was word of the death of a 21-year-old neighbour. The postman could not bring himself to deliver the letter to the bereaved mother alone. Tearfully, he begged my grandmother to accompany him. I would have been too young to understand why the women and the postman were all sobbing and hugging each other, a scene that was playing out all too frequently in many parts of the world at the time.

I remember nothing about the interior of my home in the early years other than two utility grade chairs either side of the fireplace in the sitting room. They were called easy chairs but were anything but easy. The arms were square and rigid and formed an uncomfortable obstacle to my dancing with Anne Driver. We only ever sat on them on the rare occasions the fire was lit in the sitting room—the custom in most British households.

In almost every house built until the early part of the last century, there were fireplaces in every room including the bedrooms where a fire could be lit if someone was confined there through illness. Keeping two fires going, though, was both arduous work and expensive which explains why "Ol' Robinson" was relegated to the kitchen for the last years of his life.

Fuel for the kitchen fire was collected from the surrounding woods, but the coal man would deliver big bags of coal every few months. I was always fascinated but a little frightened of the coal man as he struggled down the path to the coal house, bending under the heavy weight of the brown sack of coal on his back, only his dust reddened eyes visible in his blackened face.

Beside the fire was an oven with a heavy metal latch to open and close it. To the left of the fireplace and above the oven was what were called hobs where sat the soot blackened kettle and a similarly soot encrusted tea-pot, constantly filled with stewed black tea.

Meals were cooked there too, although often the pots would be placed right on top of the fire. When the wood or coal moved, the kettle or pot might fall over, pouring the contents into the fire with a great sizzle, producing thick, black smoke and a covering of ash. Then there would be the usual kerfuffle while someone tried to retrieve the pot and the remains of the dinner, burning his or her hands in the process. We probably ate more than our fair share of charcoal and ash along with our meals, but in those days, no one knew about carcinogens or the effects they might be having on our health. Despite that, many of my relatives and neighbours seemed to live well into their eighties and nineties.

Baking must have been quite a challenge. Knowing just how much fuel to put on the fire to arrive at the right temperature so that the oven contents did not come out partially raw or cooked beyond recognition took some judgement.

In later years, the fireplace was replaced with an Aga cooker, but even that was challenging. On a visit to Wales, my husband and I would discover just how difficult it was as the oven temperature soared to 800 degrees, and we had to resort to roasting a chicken with both the oven and kitchen doors wide open to the elements. Little wonder that the British have a reputation for cooking things to death.

Our part of the house was furnished with our own personal W.C., and it was attached to the house which saved us walking any great distance. Newspaper served as toilet paper and when that supply was exhausted, we had to resort to *The Farmers' Weekly* which was of rather a glossy nature. It would be years before Bronco and Izal made it to Tregare. Those commercial varieties came on fancy rolls which, to us, seemed so sophisticated and refined but, disappointingly, were only marginally softer or as effective as *The Farmers'*

Weekly.

The outhouse excrement was collected in a large bucket which, when full, had to be emptied and the contents buried in the woods—a job that required strength which, thankfully, it took me some years to attain. Our method, though distasteful, was rather more genteel than letting the detritus run freely out of the back of the outhouse and down a bank into a ditch which was the case at my grandparents' outhouse. There, the chickens and ducks, which were free to run around the yard and often right into the house, had a field day scratching through the human faeces and cleaning themselves off on the ash heap in front of the coal shed, giving a whole new connotation to free-range eggs.

During the night, a container was always placed in a central position—the earliest form of en-suite plumbing. I often wondered how the Johnson family managed without "a pot to piss in." In more up-market homes, the receptacle was normally a flowered, made in England, china chamber pot, now a collector's item, but in our case, a metal bucket served the same purpose and was easier to carry out without spillage in the morning. The net gain, though, was minimal; it might even have been a net loss because, too often, someone stumbling around in the darkness during the night would kick the bucket. At my grandparents' home, the bucket was foolishly kept at the top of the stairs.

The galvanized bath, which was brought in on rare occasions, hung on the outside wall of the house. Filling it was a laborious process involving the heating of many pots of water on the fire and pouring them into the bath with an equal amount of cold water. No one ever experienced the luxury of bathing in more than three inches of tepid water, and the galvanized surface, along with the overpowering smell of Lifebuoy soap, discouraged any lengthy lounging. Bathing was neither a popular nor common occurrence. It is probably the reason why my grandparents never seemed to bother with it.

Except for drinking water, rainwater was collected in large galvanized tanks which sat beside the house and were filled with the run-off from the roof. Drinking water came from a little pool fed by a spring, about half a mile away across the fields. As I grew older, it was one of my jobs to take the bucket to fill at the spring. By the time I got home, the bucket was never more than half full.

It was obviously quite an art managing to fill the bucket without the addition of a little extra protein in the form of water bugs and flies.

The spring was protected by a gate to a short path. If someone forgot to shut the gate, the animals would see their chance and trundle in. The water then became a deep yellow or dark, muddy green colour—rather less pure than what is demanded by today's exacting health standards. But, if I had my choice, I think I would settle for a few water bugs and sheep turds over the chemical concoction that I am forced to consume in my old age.

Doing the laundry was a chore that took Herculean effort; it was an entire day event. A large copper boiler with a fireplace underneath, in the corner of my grandmother's back kitchen, was our washing machine. The fire had to be lit to heat the water and the clothes were then added and boiled for several hours. Meanwhile, steam, dampness and the smell of wet washing mixed with acrid smoke escaping from the fire, permeated the whole house. A washboard was used for rubbing clothes such as shirt collars that were badly stained. Everything then had to be removed from the boiler and rinsed by hand. Whites were soaked in a blue solution to make them whiter—an exercise in futility if ever there was. The clothes were then put through the mangle which was a sizeable contraption that stood outside on wrought iron legs and had two wooden drums, turned by a metal handle, through which the clothes were fed to remove the excess water—and, inadvertently, crush most of the buttons—before being hung on the line.

During the winter, the clothes often froze, becoming as stiff as boards, so it was a fight to remove them and bring them back into the house where the ice melted, the water dripped on the floor, and we were forced to don our Wellington boots.

Ironing was a task that had to be seen to be believed. A heavy flat iron was heated up in the fire and then any ash or coal cleaned off to prevent the clothes being marked. That was virtually impossible, and since it was also impossible to control the temperature, most of our clothes ended up with black smears and singe marks or, more often than not, were completely ruined.

Things improved immeasurably with the purchase of a metal shoe that was placed over the iron. The metal shoe had probably been invented years before it arrived in Tregare, but when it did finally appear, we felt as if we had truly entered the modern era.

Paraffin fuelled the lamps which provided light in the kitchen and living room and was always delivered to the house by "The Paraffin Man." The lamps were Tilley lamps with mantles which were hopelessly impractical—fragile and likely to disintegrate at the slightest touch. There never seemed to be a spare mantle when that happened, so we were reduced to burning candles if they were available, sitting in darkness or going to bed early.

All British houses were cold to the point of extreme discomfort. The only place to get warm was right in front of the fire with feet firmly placed on the fender. Everyone, therefore, sported bright red, mottled legs from sitting too close to the flames. Chilblains, caused by cold and dampness, were a curse. Almost everyone suffered from them at some time.

The rest of the house was bitterly cold, and in the

winter a thick coating of ice covered the inside of every window and had to be scraped off each morning so that one could see outside. Any water left in the sink overnight was frozen solid by morning.

However, did we keep warm? Well, certainly a lot more underwear was worn: woollen vests and liberty bodices were the order of the day under a few layers of knitted woollen garments. I suspect most people, like my family, wore their underwear to bed.

Some were known to wear *all* their clothes to bed so that they would not have to suffer the excruciating discomfort of getting dressed in the morning. In other places, in another time, children were sewn into their undergarments at the beginning of winter and cut out of them when spring came. As unsanitary as that might sound, it certainly would have led to more bearable winters.

MEMOIR OF "A SLOPPY, SPINELESS, CREATURE"

CHAPTER FOUR

"Tell me and I forget,
Show me and I remember,
Involve me and I understand."
Chinese Proverb

I was only four years old when I set off on my educational journey to the village school.

Tregare School was built in 1875, on high ground above Raglan. Records say that it was built for the princely sum of £1,307—around $2000 and the well, which is still there, in the middle of the playground, cost £6—approximately $10 to sink.

Tregare School showing the well in the centre

The school would serve generations of children for over a hundred years, until it closed in 1977. By the time I entered the school, I believe that my father had disappeared completely, and my mother had already begun divorce proceedings—exceedingly unusual in the nineteen forties and never accepted by the Catholic Lynches as, naturally,

"God does not recognize divorce."

If, as my grandmother feared, the neighbours were still gossiping about the shotgun wedding, you can bet your life that they were having a field day with this new development.

Growing up as a child of divorced parents, in any circumstances, is upsetting, but my grandmother's continued condemnation of my father, in terms that were so coarse, hardly helped to ameliorate my situation. The divorce set me apart from other children and would, as I grew up, cause me years of misery.

As my mother had to find work, she became employed as the school cook, a position that she would hold temporarily and subsequently return to for 27 years.

Haydn had already been at Tregare School for four years, so we ambled along together. The journey was a 20-minute brisk walk for an adult, but grown-ups, with their worries and time restraints, don't have to wade through puddles, swing around signposts, feed handfuls of grass to goats pushing their bony little heads through a five-barred gate, listen to baby lambs bleating and birds singing, scuff through mounds of fallen leaves in autumn, take in the scent of violets and primroses in spring or stamp on the tar bubbles seeping up from the road surface on a hot summer's day. With so much to explore and experience, our journey, in all seasons, could take hours.

The school was isolated from any other buildings, surrounded by sheep-dotted fields which dropped away from the back, affording picturesque views towards Monmouth and the distant hills beyond. Of course, I did not appreciate the idyllic setting until I had lived abroad and returned after many years to "The Green, Green Grass of Home." Tom's rendition never fails to bring tears to my eyes.

The school yard was accessed through impressive, decorative wooden gates outside of which was a rockery filled, in the spring, with a tangle of blue periwinkle, a scene that I recall every time I see those delicate little flowers.

It was only a short walk to the school entrance, an enormous wooden double door with a thick black metal ring which had to be turned to lift the heavy latch on the inside.

Even using two hands, I wasn't strong enough to lift that latch. In one of my recurring nightmares, how often I stood outside that massive door, frantic that I would not be able to get inside.

That door led into a gloomy, windowless, cloakroom with a cold, tiled floor, coat racks lining the walls, a single classroom door on either side and the kitchen at the far end.

The playground was large enough to accommodate hundreds of children—records say that it was built to accommodate 96—excessive for such a rural school where there had never been more than 65 students at any one time. At the lower end of the playground was an enormous vegetable garden, a necessary addition during wartime—cultivated and planted by the older students.

Once a year, the mobile dentists' van arrived and parked in the lane outside. It was dark green, enormous and foreboding. Its arrival filled us all with terror and laid the foundation for a lifetime fear of dentists for all who were dragged within.

How can I forget the acrid smell of gas and the feeling of suffocation as a metal clamp was jammed into my mouth to force it open while a heavy anaesthetizing rubber mask was slapped completely over my face? Almost as unpleasant was the customary dose of castor oil that my grandmother dished out to me the night before. I still fail to see the connection between teeth removal and bowels.

Teeth were only taken out in those days, not filled—often for no good reason. My mother and all her siblings had had all their teeth removed by the age of 20. False teeth, often ill-fitting, were considered normal though, unlike my grandmother, people tended to persevere with them, rather than keep them in a jar behind the sewing machine.

British dentists had the well-deserved reputation of being the worst in the world. My husband, in his youth, was a patient at the practice of Messrs. Pullar and Payne—an ironic but reasonably accurate commentary on the entire British dental profession at the time.

On my initial visit to a Canadian dentist, I began to splutter that I had just emigrated from England, but the dentist, without waiting for me to finish, took a cursory glance in my mouth and scoffed,

"You don't have to tell me, it's obvious where you've come from."

All children entered regular day school at age four to five years of age. I was just a few days short of my fourth birthday when I entered full-time school.

No child went home for lunch. Hot meals were cooked in the school kitchen which was normal in British schools. What did we eat? I can only vividly remember the desserts, but I suspect that the menu did not vary much from the one at our house and most of the other houses in the area.

A large roast was delivered by "Ol' Jones, the meat," every Friday afternoon, and refrigerated on a stone slab in the pantry until Sunday—in the case of the school, Monday.

That roast of beef or lamb then appeared every day, in different forms, until Friday when it had been stretched far beyond the limits of possibility. Then we ate 'toad in the hole'—a revolting concoction of sausages in batter, or whatever came in a tin—corned beef or spam. Spam fritters were very popular. There was no shortage of vegetables; they came directly from the garden at the bottom of the playground. The desserts?—sago, rice pudding, tapioca, steamed puddings, treacle tart and spotted dick all smothered in custard. Ooh!—I loved them all. Alas! I still do.

The meals were cooked on a stove fuelled by propane, the smell of which almost suffocated one on entering through those heavy wooden doors, and permeated throughout the whole building mingling with the noxious smells of unwashed bodies, overcooked cabbage, chalk and Jeyes Fluid.

Even through the years of rationing, during and after the war, a third of a pint bottle of milk was provided for each child. Unpasteurized, it came with an inch of thick cream on the surface and tasted like real milk. In winter, it was warmed beside the pot-bellied stove—the only source of heating. Even though we had milking cows at home, no one ever thought of drinking their milk, but the warmed school milk tasted so delicious and so comforting.

Numbers fluctuated at the school, but there were only eleven students in two rooms with two teachers when I was in attendance. There had been several evacuees earlier on, but by September of 1945, they had all returned to their families in London.

The headmaster, Mr. Jim Williams, a stick-insect of a man with bushy eyebrows and a similar amount of hair growing out of his nostrils but rather less on his head, taught the older students in the bigger room.

In his well-worn suit, rumpled shirt and gravy and custard stained tie, Mr. Williams held forth from his perch on the edge of his old, oak desk. Peering suspiciously over his horn-rimmed spectacles, he endeavoured to fill the heads of the unwilling with facts that generally went in one ear and out the other. He always sat bolt upright, his left leg cocked over the right knee, only leaning perilously forward to make a point or ridicule a student who had given a wrong answer. Building self-esteem was not his strength. In fact, he seemed hell-bent on snuffing out any tiny spark that glimmered.

He was particularly scathing of the bigger boys, and I was under the impression that all boys were "dullards." I wasn't quite sure what a "dullard" was, but I knew it wasn't something to be proud of.

On one memorable occasion, one of the "dullards," Ray Gwilliam, reading aloud to Mr. Williams, pronounced the word "Egypt" as "eggy put." The reaction was extreme. Leaping up from the desk, Mr. Williams began to march around the room banging a ruler on the desks and clipping several boys across the back of the head:

"Eggy put? eggy put? you stupid boy! Dear Lord, deliver me from these imbeciles."

His rage continued to gain momentum as he flew into Mrs. Powell's room to report on Raymond's unbelievable level of stupidity, thence to the kitchen where my amazed mother was quietly peeling potatoes.

Returning to a room silenced by the assault, he grabbed me from my seat, ordering me to go to the front of the room to read to the class. The humiliation of Raymond was not yet over. Nor mine as it turned out.

Mr. Williams may have been proud to demonstrate my superior reading skills to the older students but, from then on, they treated me like a snotty little upstart—they really made me pay for it. They couldn't have known that I was bleeding inside for poor Raymond.

After all, what could a boy who had grown up in the narrow confines of Tregare be expected to know of Egypt? He probably could have told Mr. Williams the gestation period of a mare, how a cow's stomach works and the difference between wheat and barley. He probably knew how to shear a sheep, plough a field and stick a pig, but in school he was left in no doubt that he was "as thick as two short planks," poor little sod.

Compared to the parents of his students, Mr.

Williams had a very soft number indeed. Country schools came with impressive houses attached where the headmaster lived free of charge or for a minimal rent—undoubtedly a plan to lure teachers to those isolated rural schools.

Sometimes, there were as few as four students in Mr. Williams's room so he was never inconvenienced by a burdensome workload. Being a heavy smoker, he liked to get the children out to play as often and for as long as possible. Once turned into the playground, his charges realized that, mostly, they could get away with murder.

Mrs. Powell taught the younger children in the smaller room. It really was a small room and the pot-bellied stove made it cosy and welcoming.

Every day, Mrs. Powell rode up from Raglan, a village three miles distant, on her rickety old bicycle. Mrs. Powell was neither German nor gypsy, but she wore heavy makeup and earrings and painted her fingernails and toenails vivid red to match her lipstick. Not only that, she bleached her hair white blond, wore very short skirts—a titillating site on a bicycle, and, heaven forbid!—perfume!

To me she was the princess in all the old familiar fairy stories, and I imagined she lived in a castle, but my grandmother called her a floozy, said she smelled like a whore and was only interested in S E X. By age four, I had mastered three letter words, but that did not deter my grandmother from continuing to spell out words that were not considered fit for my ears until I left home at the age of eighteen.

Mrs. Powell sat behind a very tall desk in front of the class. We sat facing her in a row of little wooden desks with seats attached. There was an indentation at the top of the desk for pens and pencils and a china inkwell in a hole on the right at the top for ink.

Initially, we wrote with chalk on slates, but quickly we graduated to writing in exercise books with ink—a very messy business indeed. It was only possible to write one or two words before the pen had to be dipped again, by which time we had often smudged our work with our sleeves. Then Mrs. Powell would laugh and say,

"This looks just like a dog's breakfast."

Everyone was provided with a sheet of pink blotting paper, but the older students taught us that the best use of that was to dip pieces in the inkwell and make ink balls to fire at other children.

Mrs. Powell called us up to her desk to read to her. I loved the orange and black characters in my *Happy Venture* first reader—Dick and Dora, their cat, Fluff, and dog, Nip, who engaged in all the stimulating activities that could be achieved with the use of three letter words. It didn't take much to make me happy. I loved school and I adored Mrs. Powell, and although I did not appreciate it at the time, she taught me everything that I needed to know and would continue to need and enjoy in my adult life.

She introduced me to the magical world of books. A tiny bookcase with two shelves in Mr. Williams's room housed our complete library. Once a month, a van arrived with a few replacements. Amongst other favourites, I was a fan of *Milly, Molly, Mandy*, and I was filled with excitement when a new one in the series appeared on the shelf. Her real name was Millicent Margaret Amanda and she wore a pink and white striped dress. I longed to look just like her and have an impressive name like that. Those of us who had mastered reading gobbled up the few new books in days and then, knowing that we would have to wait four long weeks for a new batch, would reread them repeatedly until we had almost committed them to memory.

Mrs. Powell instilled in us the joy of nature and growing things. She created a vegetable garden especially for the younger students, involving us at every step. She taught us how to prepare the ground and plant seeds. She emphasized the importance of composting to replenish the soil and when and how to harvest the crops. We were encouraged to eat the salad goods we grew, and the root vegetables were taken to my mother in the kitchen to be used in our school dinners.

Combating globalization and reducing carbon footprints were not on the radar, and no one had need to experiment with the Hundred Mile Diet. We trod so lightly upon the earth and were all, by necessity, involved in a less than ten metre diet, both at home and in school. How sad it is that in progressing, we have regressed almost beyond the point of no return in just two generations—a mere blink in our earth's history.

I learned to knit using a pair of green bone needles and some bright yellow, soft cotton yarn. I became attached like a limpet to that piece of knitting and felt its silkiness lovingly as stitch by painful stitch it grew into what I dreamed would be a scarf, though the width varied wildly and the dropped stitches produced holes as big as the old English halfpennies.

To my dismay, once I had mastered the skill, Mrs. Powell took my yellow knitting and green bone needles away to teach another younger child to knit. Devastated, I watched with envy while the other little girl massacred my work. What I did not understand was that there was so little money for supplies during and following the war that the yellow wool and the one pair of needles was all that my teacher had to work with. I was blissfully unaware of what now would be seen as deficiencies. It is only when one lives in a world of super-abundance that a lack of material things becomes of any consequence.

Much to my joy, Mrs. Powell embraced Anne Driver, so I could continue leaping about to her music while Mrs. Powell demonstrated the actions, her skirt and her bleached blond hair flying with gay abandon. I was thankful that my grandmother was never witness to those performances.

She was way off base in her assessment of Mrs. Powell's interests. She referred to her as "That ol' Mrs. Powell,"—old not meaning age—Mrs. Powell must have been all of 20 years old at the time—but a derogatory term employed for many people of whom my grandmother disapproved, including the deceased Mr. Robinson.

Normally, I would have stayed in Mrs. Powell's protective care until I was seven years old, but when older children became of age to move on to the Secondary Modern School in Monmouth leaving Mr. Williams with only a couple of students, a few of the younger ones had to be promoted so that he could continue to justify his position and his house. This move, which initially filled me with trepidation, exceeded my wildest dreams.

Every afternoon, if the weather cooperated, Mr. Williams announced, as if it was a rare treat,

"Well, I think we will do a spot of gardening this afternoon."

Out we tripped, first to the vegetable garden but very quickly into his own private garden where we dug, weeded and raked. We were all farm children—strong as oxen, able and used to demanding work. We kept that garden in tip-top shape while Mr. Williams spent leisurely afternoons enjoying a 'fag', leaning over the wall admiring the view of the Welsh hills.

The only person who became a little nervous about the arrangement was my mother. In conversation with Mrs. Bradley, she concluded that I was not going to get far in life unless my ambition was to become a labourer. The Bradley children had all bypassed Tregare in favour of what their mother thought were better schools in Monmouth.

Mrs. Bradley felt that she was a cut above the neighbours and had ambition for her brood. Under her influence, my mother began to make rumblings to remove me from the school, a plan of which I was not at all in favour. Who amongst us would not love the relaxed learning environment, the daily gardening sessions and the lengthy playtimes?

Many of our games were like those played today— hopscotch, football, skipping, tag, marbles and jacks, but in late spring it was always conkers. Conkers, the seeds of the mighty horse-chestnut trees, were gathered with such excitement every year. Many of them fell in their prickly, green, outer coating. I loved to remove the shiny, copper brown seeds from their cream-coloured, fleshy beds.

The game was vicious and made much more so when the big boys taught us how to bake the seeds in the oven to make them even harder. Putting a conker on a string, the idea was to knock another child's off its string. Black eyes, cuts and bruises were par for the course. A smack from one of those hard conkers could have knocked someone unconscious, but parents and teachers did not interfere in our games, and we were oblivious to the danger.

I try to imagine a game like that being allowed in schools today. Children are currently so overprotected by parents and teachers alike that they are often, for fear of injury, banned from engaging in simple, innate activities like running and climbing. In the last Canadian school at which I taught, balls were declared dangerous weapons and banned.

Due to the ingenuity of the older children, we were easily coerced into situations that we knew would get us into hot water.

A favourite game was hide-and-seek in the air-raid shelter. Being in such an isolated part of the country, far from cities, we were fortunate that it had never been needed for its intended purpose, but it provided us with an interesting addition to our play area, even though it was strictly out of bounds.

MEMOIR OF "A SLOPPY, SPINELESS, CREATURE"

We understood little of the seriousness of war but enacted our own wars, donning the gas masks that every child had been issued during the war, and creeping around in the darkness, throwing "hand grenades" and taking each other prisoner, dragging each other "behind enemy lines."

The most daring game was escaping into the adjoining field to hunt for rabbits. Scores of them hopped about near the school wall before a cruel disease, myxomatosis, was introduced from Australia in 1953 and killed them all.

Choosing a rabbit warren, one boy would light a match to newspaper and stuff it down one of the holes to smoke out the rabbits, while others waited to pounce on any that escaped, and the younger students kept watch. I don't remember if any rabbits were ever captured, but I do remember what happened to us when we were finally caught in the act.

Finding the playground devoid of children, one day, and getting no response when he rang the bell repeatedly, Mr. Williams was eventually forced to clamber over the wall and stumble across the field to retrieve us. This was prior to Raymond Gwilliams's faux pas over "eggy put," so I had not yet witnessed this side of our headmaster—purple in the face, panting for breath and spluttering with anger. Back in the school, he lined us all up in the cloakroom and produced his cane.

"This is going to hurt me more than it will hurt you," he lied before going down the line, whipping each one of us on the hand six times. A notorious boy—Dai Thomas, made the serious error of pulling his hand away at the crucial moment, and for that he got six more harder applications—a lesson to the rest of us quickly learned.

That was the first time I had been caned—I was not more than six years old, but canings for misdemeanours were not uncommon and it was meant to hurt. There was a rumour that the pain could be reduced by putting hairs from the coconut-hair doormat across the palm of the hand so we all tried it to no effect.

I continued to be blissfully happy at school, despite the canings, which were probably well deserved. I felt much safer there than I did at home, and I daydreamed that Mrs. Powell would, one day, carry me off to her castle. Since she only had a bicycle, I don't think I had quite figured out the logistics of the transportation.

The only thing that eventually would cause me any unhappiness was Gracie Thomas's determination to make me pay for Raymond's humiliation. She had a habit of waiting at the outhouses, blocking the door to prevent me from going in. Once she had achieved her goal, making me wet my knickers, or worse, she teased me unmercifully.

We did not refer to such behaviour as bullying in those days. In our turn, we all teased the more vulnerable children. One skinny little girl who smelled even riper than the rest of us was known as "Stinking Biffy." I have often wondered if Stinking Biffy ever managed to overcome that hard knock to her self-esteem.

The discussion about my move to another school continued for another year. My mother had difficulty plucking up the courage to broach the subject with Mr. Williams, knowing how upset he would be to lose one of his eleven pupils, not to mention his star digger and raker.

The concern was that in a few more years I would have to take the Eleven-Plus exam which would determine my path in life. Mr. Williams assured my mother that I would pass with flying colours, but since no student from Tregare had done so in living memory, she knew my chances were not promising.

When she finally went ahead with the arrangements to transfer me to a Monmouth school at the age of nine, I was convinced that my life was over.

Whether my mother had done me a favour would remain to be seen.

CHAPTER FIVE

"The simple things are also the most extraordinary things, and only the wise can see them."
Paulo Coelho

Along with my early education came my religious education. Every Sunday, Haydn and I, and other neighbourhood children walked the mile and a half to Sunday School at St. Mary's church along Park Lane. With the departure of my father, I had to abandon the left footers' camp and, at the tender age of four and a half, I became a practising Anglican.

We set off always with our grandmother's dire warning not to pick flowers. It was a neighbour girl, Sheila Hale, who had been bitten by an adder while gathering primroses in Park Lane, and, although she had lived, she had, according to my grandmother's assessment, "gone funny in the head" as a result. Concerned that we might suffer a similar fate, we were keen to heed the warnings.

Tregare Church as seen from the "new" churchyard

St. Mary's church is an ancient stone building of the Early English style dating back to 1751. All the records of family births, marriages and deaths can be found there.

The Reverend Phillips, who, to my eyes was as old as Methuselah but probably wasn't much more than 45 years old, conducted the Sunday School classes. He had a split personality, the kinder half of which he did everything in his power to conceal from children.

Outside of the church, he was quite a jovial individual who enjoyed nothing better than a good joke. Inside the church, he unveiled a different persona entirely. To us, he was a miserable individual, thin and bent with a pinched face and rheumy eyes behind wire-rimmed glasses through which he surveyed us with obvious disdain.

Dressed for sermons to the congregation from the pulpit, he always looked so well put together in snowy white robes, but we didn't seem to warrant such fancy togs. For us, at Sunday School, he wore a faded and mouldy, food-stained, black cassock that had seen better days and had undergone more than a few vicious attacks by moths.

He was hardly the kind of messenger that I think God would have desired. He preached of a being who was all fire and brimstone, and he led us to believe that God was waiting in the wings to smite us for the smallest of transgressions. There was no God of love presiding over Tregare. We were all terrified both of him and the Reverend Phillips.

Apart from scaring us out of our wits, he bellowed at adults in attendance at the Sunday services seemingly blaming the devout few for the multitude of absent sinners.

I was quite accustomed to abuse so, despite his tirades, I loved Sunday School for: the familiar Bible stories, the wonderful hymns and the special times in the church year.

Most memorable was the Harvest Festival when the ladies of the community brought their contributions to decorate the church—a profusion of flowers, fruit, vegetables and grains. Walking into that ancient building on the evening of the service, one was overcome by the mellow, ripe smells of a bountiful harvest mingling with the burning of candle wax and the musty smell of centuries. The oil lamps were lit, casting a warm glow over the faces of the congregation waiting humbly in the hard, wooden pews entwined with old man's beard. As each new person entered, the candles flickered, casting shadows that danced like spirits around the walls. In front of the dimly lit altar lay an oversized loaf of bread, shaped like a wheat sheaf, surrounded by piles of rosy red apples and golden yellow marrows of all shapes and sizes.

An unearthly warmth in that unheated, normally icy-cold building penetrated the hearts of the believers. This was the one time in the year that the bells rang out, the church was filled to capacity, and the sound of singing of those wonderful harvest hymns could be heard for miles around, reverberating across the hills and valleys:

"We Plough the Fields and Scatter the Good Seed on the Land," and my favourite,

"To Thee oh Lord our Hearts We Raise in Hymns of Adoration." It was the only time of the year that I believed that God might actually be a benevolent sort.

Aunt Maisie, weak chest temporarily on hold, would be furiously pedalling away on the old harmonium as she hammered out the hymns. My grandfather in his role as churchwarden, would be handing around the collection plate and my grandmother would be there with her teeth, unable to sing too lustily for fear of losing them, while keeping a beady eye on the congregation so that she could make snide comments about her neighbours following the service.

Apart from the Sunday lessons, there were related events to which we looked forward every year—the Annual Christmas Party, the Summer Picnic—usually held in one of the fields at Oakdale.

The Sunday School Picnic with the Reverend Phillips. I am in front, second from the right.

No one, other than the Bradley family, ever celebrated birthdays with parties, and in our house, no one even acknowledged birthdays. I grew up not really knowing when my birthday was, so, other than Guy Fawkes Night, Christmas, and an occasional holiday with Aunt Blodwen when she was in desperate need of covert sex, those three events were the highlights of our year.

The Christmas party took place in the church hall with a decorated Christmas tree, holly and mistletoe and festoons of home-made, paper chains crisscrossing the room above our heads. We welcomed the Reverend Phillips's spirited grandchildren, Michael and David who always came up from Cardiff for the parties, injecting new life and mischief into the proceedings.

We played musical chairs, blind-man's-bluff, postman's knock and pass-the-parcel and then Father Christmas—always my grandfather, clothed in a tattered, moth-eaten old costume with lumps of cotton wool hanging off it in shreds—handed out the presents. I don't think anyone was fooled into thinking he was the real thing.

The present was always a suitably chosen book which was received with such pleasure and, in my case, read avidly within the next couple of days. We then ate our favourite food—jelly and blancmange, fairy cakes and Swiss roll and washed it all down with copious amounts of tea—absolute heaven!

During August, we were taken by bus to Barry Island or Porthcawl. It was a special occasion for which we all wore our Sunday best. My grandfather always got togged up in his best suit and his collar and tie.

A daring move indeed—my grandfather has removed his trilby hat on the beach.

Our excitement, as we gathered to board that bus,

was short-lived. Before we reached Marble Hall, five minutes away, the first child, unused to travelling in a vehicle of any kind and overcome by diesel fumes would vomit, the smell of which would turn a few more stomachs and an array of buckets would be passing around the bus before we had gone more than a few miles.

Barry Island was paradise to us with its stretch of sandy beach, the sea in which to bathe—no one had ever had an opportunity to learn to swim—soggy tomato sandwiches and a flask of tea on the cliffs, and a real funfair with sideshows, penny machines and thrilling rides.

Barry Island always seemed to be the place where members of the family were photographed, perhaps because cameras were rare, and few people owned them.

It was quite a novelty to us when Aunt Blodwen arrived at Oakdale with her first Brownie Box model. Eastman Kodak had introduced the concept of the snapshot to the masses as early as 1900, but it would be over 40 years before such advanced technology would appear in our part of the world.

My grandmother, Aunt Phyllis, Haydn, and I to the left. The Morgan family to the right. Two families sharing the cost of a professional photographer in Barry Island

The day always ended with the ultimate treat—fish and chips in newspaper—hardly a wise choice for a group of children with weak stomachs about to board the bus home.

Before we left the outskirts of Barry Island, the buckets would be out again to receive the half-digested remains of the fish and chips, and the noise of retching and the smell of vomit would accompany us all the way home.

My charcoal lined stomach always held me in good stead. I would soon drift off to sleep dreaming of the wonderful experience we had enjoyed.

Immanuel Kant once said,

"We are not rich by what we possess but by what we can do without."

One of the greatest advantages of growing up in rural Wales during and following the war was that we were poor without having the slightest idea that we were. Certainly, our activities and experiences may seem very limited by today's standards, but, in so many ways, were more precious and rich for their rarity.

I feel privileged to remember Christmas as it used to be. Although I received very little in the way of material gifts, the anticipation and joy were no less intense.

As Christmas approached, it was a tradition to go carol singing around the neighbourhood. Adults and children piled onto a cart filled with hay bales and drawn by one of the Bradley's tractors—driven by Walter and supplied with enough bottles of homemade cider to keep him lubricated throughout the evening.

With frost glittering on the ground and the stars twinkling overhead, we chugged along to the cottages and farms. How could I ever forget the year that flakes of snow were falling gently upon us as we sang by the dim light of my grandfather's hurricane lamp?

About two weeks before Christmas, Haydn and I would go in search of a tree. Park Wood, behind the house, was still mostly deciduous at that time, so it was never an easy task to find a suitable evergreen tree. Even though it might take several days, we were never disappointed. With what pride we dragged home that tree—usually a yew—and with what excitement we placed it in an old metal bucket of earth in the corner of my grandparents' kitchen. It was an apology for a tree compared to the magnificent cultured specimens of today, but to us it was always just perfect.

During the days that followed, we spent our time making decorations—bells from cardboard, covered with gold and silver paper saved all year from cigarette packet wrappings, and paper chains and stars made of old white envelopes and coloured with crayons. A larger piece of gold or silver paper was saved for the star at the top of the tree.

I don't know if commercial decorations were even available then, but if they were, we were not aware of them and certainly could not have afforded them. In any case, we took such pleasure in making our own. Since there was no electricity, real candles were then placed on the tree—a potentially dangerous practice in our house where missile assault was as frequent as bombs dropping on London.

Our stockings—my grandmother's used, thick Lisle ones—it would be many years before DuPont nylon reached Tregare—were filled with inexpensive little gifts. There was always a mandarin in the toe, the only time in the year that we ever saw one. Delivered stealthily in the night, the stockings were left on the foot of the bed where that glorious heaviness weighed across our feet on Christmas morning.

The gifts under the tree were picked up, squeezed, turned over and smelled continually for days before Christmas in the same way that in future years I would see my own children and grandchildren doing. Like them, we wanted so desperately to know what was in the packages but, at the same time, did not wish to spoil the surprise.

I always guessed I would get an Enid Blyton book and an annual—*The Rupert Bear Annual*, or, when I was older, *The Girls' Crystal Annual.* I loved Rupert Bear in his red sweater, yellow check pants and matching scarf, and the little rhymes that appeared under every picture. I can still conjure up those books in my mind, smell their newness and remember the sheer joy of being able to disappear into a corner to read the stories and do the puzzles all day long.

There were other gifts too—mittens, socks, underwear, a box of crisp white cotton handkerchiefs, a board game—Snakes and Ladders or Ludo, a box of pencil crayons that came with a pencil sharpener and always a special, more expensive gift from Aunt Blodwen—a paint by number set with little pots of real oil paint, the smell of which still lingers on my memory, a doll or, once, a teddy-bear that 71 years later, I still possess. Each year, I would take my little pile of gifts to place beside my bed and look at it lovingly, rearranging it repeatedly.

Titles of books that I received each year, both at home and at the Sunday School party, are etched forever in my memory: *Heidi, Little Women, A Peep Behind the Scenes, A Christmas Carol.*

I wonder if we are allowing today's children to experience the same kind of pleasure? Perhaps it is of little importance but, to me, childhood memories of simple joy form the foundation on which our future lives are built.

A memoir is just what it is meant to be—an accurate account of one's life. One should not be passing judgement in any way, but it is difficult, in an age of such excess, not to compare the simplicity of life and the satisfaction given by small things, only two generations past, with the gross consumerism of today.

In December 2013 when I was 72 years old, my husband, John, was listening to a podcast—*The Degrowth Paradigm*. The speaker, Richard Swift, was exploring a more modest and sane alternative to the constant pressures of expansion that are destroying the ecological basis of our existence.

"Ah," commented I smugly, "They are speaking about the need to return to the kind of life we old people were privileged to experience 70 or more years ago."

MEMOIR OF "A SLOPPY, SPINELESS, CREATURE"

CHAPTER SIX

"A well-developed sense of humour is the pole that adds balance to your step as you walk the tightrope of life." William Arthur Ward

A large country estate which we called "The Mansion," only a mile from Oakdale, housed young men who had returned from the trenches and were assigned to the farms that had been largely neglected during the war years. There they were trained in the skills of farming and market gardening. The place provided more lucrative employment for my mother and two of her sisters, but it was on a live-in basis, so my grandmother then became our sole caregiver. I use that word loosely.

At this point, my mother and I moved into my grandparents' part of the house, although the rental of the bungalow continued, and we used the sitting room there on rare, special occasions, such as Christmas Day. There, the cold and dampness could not be masked even by the heat of a roaring fire, most of which went straight up the chimney.

There were no easy chairs in my grandparents' home. That would have smacked of leisure—another name for idleness—not to be encouraged at any cost. The living room which was also the kitchen was furnished with a large oil-cloth covered table and six or seven hard-backed wooden chairs. Other than those, there was a sideboard for housing the sewing machine and the teeth jar, an ancient piano and an even older harmonium, suggesting, perhaps, a bygone hope of producing musical prodigies which had failed to materialize.

The harmonium was more of a surface on which to place a collection of deformed, dust-covered cacti that contributed nothing remotely aesthetically pleasing and served only to block out the light and get caught up on what fragments remained of the lace curtains every time they were drawn back or closed.

A binder-twine line, always full of drying washing under which it was necessary to duck, stretched from one side of the room to the other, sagging over the piano and down the backs of those unfortunates who sat on that side of the table. The walls were clad in faded wallpaper, much of it peeling from the damp. Two black and white family photographs—one of Blodwen in her nurse's uniform and the other of Philip in his army uniform—held pride of place above the piano. The only other picture portrayed a kneeling, mop-haired, angelic looking child in a white gown. It was entitled "The Maiden's Prayer"—my grandmother's prized possession—painted on glass as it was, she told us and priceless. In future years, "The Maiden's Prayer" would come to a sticky end.

The smell of soot and the thick smoke emanating from coal and wet wood constantly filled our lungs. The black-lead fireplace was surrounded by a metal guard rail which provided extra drying space, but acted as a barrier to any faint hope of warmth.

The mantelpiece above the fireplace held a collection of tawdry bric-a-brac, and from the ceiling above the oil-cloth covered table, completing the felicitous decor, hung a few fly-papers displaying the week's catch, some of which were still struggling desperately to get free. The room had a Dickensian feel to it—cold, bleak and comfortless.

So, began my life at the mercy of my unbalanced grandmother. There was much speculation in the family as to the cause of her sudden and shocking outbursts. Her daughters spoke of her being affected by the phases of the moon, and there were hushed whispers about "The C H A N G E," but if the latter had been the case, then it may have resulted in yet another opportunity for the Joneses to make it into *The Guinness Book of*

Records.

It is true that my grandmother had lived a very hard life. She had raised six children on practically nothing, finding any creative way she could to supplement the family's insufficient income. For years, every week, she had walked four miles to catch a train to get to Abergavenny market to sell whatever she could muster: vegetables, a couple of rabbits, a dressed chicken, bunches of daffodils or dyed pampas grass fronds, to earn a little cash to buy necessities for the family.

Sometimes, she would have to stand in that bitterly cold, draughty market all day waiting for someone to purchase her wares. At the end of the day, completely worn out, she would have to walk the four miles home to light the fire, cobble together a simple meal for her husband and six children, tend to the chickens, ducks and turkeys and then, perhaps, spend the evening baking or making clothes for the family.

In later years, a bus passed the house on market day which made her life considerably easier. During the school holidays, she would take us to market with her so that we could help with the heavy baskets of produce.

I did not enjoy the interminable hours standing around that frigid, dismal place, inhaling the sickly smells of rotting vegetables, over-ripe fruit, and raw meat, attempting to avoid the pools of congealing blood that had dripped from hanging animal carcasses, while my grandmother gossiped with the other vendors.

One of those was my great aunt Ellen who I only ever saw at the market—my grandmother also had four or five other sisters and a few brothers who seemed to keep their distance. I remember once hearing the news that her sister, Florrie, had died. None of us had ever met Florrie so her death was hardly a life changing event.

From their disjointed and whispered conversations, we deduced that Aunt Ellen's family was as dysfunctional as ours—so many members whose origin was unclear—so many secrets that would never be revealed.

We were always promised a toasted tea-cake and a cup of tea once everything had been sold, but my grandmother's promises were never unconditional, so we could never depend on her carrying through on them. One can exert enormous power by keeping everyone in a constant state of hope and excitement mixed with anxiety.

Very little was understood about mental illness in those days, and there was no treatment except banishment to what my grandmother herself referred to as the "loony bin" for the serious cases. There was absolutely nothing that could be done for my grandmother who unfailingly presented herself as the picture of good humour and sanity to the outside world.

We did not dare complain to anyone, and it was useless to speak to our mothers who had been brought up under similar circumstances. We suffered in silence, dealing with our internal turmoil as best we could. Those were the "grin and bear it" days without the aid of psychologists or psychiatrists.

Today, her condition might be called Intermittent Explosive Disorder or I.E.D—a mental illness marked by outbursts of uncontrollable rage. Dr. Emil Coccaro, chair of the department of psychiatry and behavioural neuroscience at the University of Chicago, believes that it affects three to five percent of the adult population. Dr. Coccaro states,

"I can guarantee you that there is nobody out there who wants to be the poster child for this disorder." Well, I can guarantee Dr. Coccaro that there is nobody out there who wants to be the poster child for the person who must live with someone suffering from the disorder.

One day, as I was relating some of my grandmother's antics to my youngest daughter, Nicola, she laughed,

"Oh Mum, you're making it up."

Memoir writers are often accused of exaggeration, but it is also said that truth is stranger than fiction. I can certainly attest to that.

My grandmother kept a thin, willow stick on the mantelpiece, a warning, mostly, to keep us in line, although she used it on the back of our legs until they were red raw on many occasions. I wore my Wellington boots to school on many a hot summer day, ashamed of the red welts on my legs. I knew I could not tell the truth when both teachers repeatedly questioned the unsuitability of my footwear, but I have since wondered if they suspected the reason.

The willow stick was by no means the worst of her cautionary devices. Her most frightening deterrent was the carving knife. She never actually stabbed us and only occasionally managed to draw blood when she threw it, because in the interest of self-preservation, we became experts at dodging the weapon, but, when provoked, she chased us around the kitchen and then pushed up the kitchen table trapping us between it and the piano threatening to kill us while screaming,

"You bloody little bastards, I'll 'ave your guts for garters," or similar, less genteel warnings.

When we were very young, we inevitably ended up trapped behind the table, terrified, while she brandished the knife inches from our necks. Through bitter experience, we became smarter and escaped through the back door with her in hot pursuit. She was a fast runner, but necessity gave us the strength to outrun her. I think I might have her to thank for my greater than average ability to run long distances in my old age.

Often, she took the carving knife under the stairs and pretended to kill herself. Blood curdling screams, for fifteen minutes or more, would be followed by a terrifying silence. Rigid with fear, we would sit on the edge of our hard-backed chairs. An hour or two later, she would emerge from the scene of her death and carry on as if nothing untoward had happened. Initially, this was the stuff of nightmares, but as we grew older and the frequency of such scenes did not abate, we realized that she was never going to have the courage to carry through on her threats. There were times when we fervently wished that she would.

On other occasions, she threatened to eat rat poison. The same routine was followed except the screams were often louder and more agonizing and the dying process extended for better effect. Then there were days when she changed the death scene from under the stairs to the woods. Off she would march in her curlers and apron—obviously with no aspiration to die looking her best—clutching the can of rat poison in her pocket. After a short interval, we would cover our ears to drown out the ear-piercing screams emanating from the woods. There was little chance of the neighbours hearing her as they all lived so far away, but although none of us ever dared speak of her outlandish behaviour, we can't be sure if any of them were aware of what occurred.

While she had managed to intimidate her own children, and was still doing so in their adulthood, she began to find it increasingly difficult to bully Haydn. Being younger, I lived through every day of my early years in a constant state of fear, but Haydn, despite his seemingly delicate demeanour, became more and more impertinent. He began to challenge her and deliberately provoke her. He seemed to develop a morbid desire to see her riled up.

The verbal abuse she heaped upon him, particularly about his illegitimacy, and the threats she issued about sending him back to live with "that scum"— his father—who lived nearby, cut me to the quick, but he acted as if it was water off a duck's back to him. How could it have been? He did have a wicked sense of humour, but I think it was just his way of protecting himself from her cruel barbs.

Rose and Haydn, inseparable—those two "little bastards"

Haydn's father always passed us on a tractor, on market days, while we were walking home from school. I felt distress on Haydn's behalf, knowing how agonizing those encounters were for him. There would never be any acknowledgement of association, only a painful reminder of the denial that they shared flesh and blood. As Haydn got older, the resemblance between them grew in proportion to our shared torment.

Throwing things was another of my grandmother's daily pastimes, but, as luck would have it, she had a terrible aim. Plates, cups, butter, saucepans full of hot water or the teapot full of scalding tea—anything that was to hand—would come hurtling through the air. Often, my poor grandfather was the intended recipient. On more than one occasion, he was goaded into a return lob. The kitchen could turn into a sporting venue in seconds, with chairs overturned, the table scraping across the floor to collide with the piano, china smashed to smithereens and food dripping from the walls and the ceiling. On one occasion, she threw an unopened two-pound bag of sugar at my grandfather. I can't remember if food rationing had ended by that time, but if it had not, there went our family's weekly allowance.

The bag hit the candlestick which was attached to the piano with such force that it exploded like a bomb. On an earlier occasion, a burning candle had caused the decorative, pleated, satin baize and part of the front of the piano to go up in flames. Much of the sugar, therefore, ended up inside the delicate workings. I'm sure Mr. Goldsmith, the piano tuner, was more than a little mystified when he next came to tune it, but being British, he acted as if it was quite normal to find the bulk of a week's sugar ration inside a piano. He just smiled politely and made no comment.

Following one of those outbursts, the clean-up of the battle scene was left to us while my grandmother took off, once more, to slit her throat under the stairs.

Everything had usually been restored to some semblance of order by the time the moaning and wailing ended. When she eventually emerged, we would endure "clouts" across the head, a good "clip" around the ear and the usual verbal profanities. I was so used to being called: a "flibberty-gibbet," a "brazen hussy," a "cheeky wench," an "impudent bitch," an "ungrateful wretch" that I imagined the list was endless.

She had several oft'-repeated sayings none of which any of us really understood. We would "rue the day." What day did she mean exactly? Was it the day we were, at last, relegated to the Workhouse? Perhaps it was the day she finally did herself in. No, we certainly wouldn't have rued that day. Could it have been Judgement Day?" We'll never know, any more than we will understand what she meant by our behaviour being "enough to surfeit a snipe," or perhaps she meant "surface a snipe." Are snipes particularly long suffering I wondered, but, if pushed to the limit, just can't take it anymore? Each night, I crept off to bed wondering about the threatened "rude awakening." So often she warned us that she was going to "read the riot act." What did she mean? As far as we were concerned, she was the sole perpetrator of riots. She frequently repeated,

"Mark my words, my girl, one of these days you are goin' to come a cropper." As a very young child, I assumed that was a prediction that I was destined to become a farmer. To me, that didn't seem to be such an awful fate as I knew that, by the age of seven, I had already acquired much of the necessary experience.

Scenes such as these were an almost daily occurrence and though disturbing, we had no choice but to tolerate them believing that, when they were over, no one would be seriously injured or killed.

Only on one occasion did I believe that Haydn surely would be—the night that she threatened to hang him with a sock. We were alone with her. The rest of the family had just left to attend a church meeting. With a murderous look in her eye she uttered in a terrifying whisper,

"This is my chance, you little bastard, while there's no one 'ere to save you. You weren't wanted in the first place and no one's goin' to miss you."

Foolishly, Haydn ran up the stairs trapping himself on the landing. Grabbing one of my grandfather's socks from the washing line and bringing the whole works down on top of the piano and the table, she bounded up the stairs after him, two at a time. I tried to scream, but no sound escaped. I ran out of the house and tore up the lane at a gallop, desperate to convey that there was trouble afoot.

"Good God Almighty, what the bloody 'ell's goin' on now? shouted my exasperated grandfather as he, my mother and Maisie turned on their heels and raced back to the house.

On their return, Aunt Maisie, true to form, managed to execute the most impressive and dramatic faint, right in the kitchen doorway, which brought everyone, including my grandmother, immediately to her aid. Haydn, grinning sheepishly, sauntered down the stairs to live for another day, and once Aunt Maisie had been revived, we all set about reattaching the binder-twine line, rehanging the washing and pretending that everything was just hunky-dory in the Jones household.

So often, our anticipation of the few special events in our lives could be ruined by my grandmother's behaviour. Suddenly, without warning, she would begin to moan and scream and pretend that she was dying.

On one occasion, as I was excitedly preparing to attend the Sunday School Christmas Party, I heard the usual commotion emanating from upstairs. Whether I had decided that I just couldn't take any more, or whether I was beginning to learn from Haydn the skilful art of calling her bluff, I cannot remember, but, shouting up to her that I would go for help, I raced down the lane, clothed only in my underwear, to alert the neighbour.

Within minutes, my grandmother was following in hot pursuit, and, because I wasn't wearing shoes, she managed to catch up with me, just as I was opening the Jones's front gate.

She hit me across the head with such force that my ears rang, and I tottered to the ground where she kicked me several times for good measure. I was threatened with the Workhouse and being returned to my drunken father, along with a host of other verbal abuse, as she marched me home where we continued with the preparations to go out.

Less than an hour later, attired in her best frock, she was bathed in Cheshire Cat smiles and charming everyone at the party as she poured the tea, while Haydn and I, once more, managed to conceal the shards of our fractured lives.

Apart from her own rages, her unequal treatment of her children caused frequent jealousies amongst them. Too often, at the tipping point of anger, a wrong word or gesture could instigate a full-blown fight. Other than Aunt Phyllis who tried to be the peacemaker in the family, the others always seemed to be at each other's throats, and often they would resort to screaming obscenities and even fist-fighting. Those fights upset me as much as my grandmother's behaviour. How I wished that I could run away to a normal family and a happier home life.

One might wonder why my mother and Aunt Phyllis did not intervene on our behalf, but because of my grandmother's all-encompassing power, we thought of them more as victims on our level rather than mothers. My grandmother ruled with a rod of iron. We, like her own children, called her Mam. More confusing for me was that my mother, being so young and completely intimidated and overruled by my grandmother, was hardly one's idea of a mother figure. To me, she was just an equal on the battlefield of insanity.

While I can now make light of my grandmother's behaviour and the never-ending brawls that shaped my early years, life, as one might imagine, was exceedingly traumatic and unpredictable. We were all constantly sitting on the edge of our seats at mealtimes expecting my grandmother to blow her stack at any minute. At the slightest provocation, something as simple as uttering a single word while she was listening to the news, plates of food would be airborne, chairs would be knocked over, abuse would be heaped upon us and yet another meal would be ruined.

Living with a woman who was frequently under the stairs going through the motions of slitting her throat, threatening to swallow rat poison and hurling china, food and verbal abuse could cause one more than a little emotional trauma. My mother and her siblings all manifested the scars of abuse in one way or another, and Haydn and I, though marginally more resilient, would spend many years of our lives dealing with our internal turmoil. For me personally, there would be added years paddling upstream against the current.

All children experience fears and nightmares at some stage in their lives, but I spent my childhood afraid to go to sleep at night because of a recurring dream. In a normal home, I could have sought comfort from an understanding adult, but in our home, no one was expected to have fears. Only weaklings suffered fears.

Nightly, I dreamt that I was cautiously walking across an enormous field of upturned pipes, trying desperately not to fall through until I reached the end of the expanse, only to slide down the last one, at breakneck speed, into a black, bottomless, pit, which awoke me trembling with fear and kept me awake for the remainder of the night.

It would have been interesting to know how a dream like that would have been interpreted by an expert, but my own interpretation was that in my life, no matter how carefully I tried to avoid disaster, things would not work out well for me in the end. For the time being, that appeared to be the path on which I trod.

Many nights I suffered terrifying attacks of profuse sweating and found myself gasping for breath, a heavy weight crushing the air from my lungs. I did not know why at the time, but I now know that I was suffering from chronic anxiety. I confided in no one but reached the point of being afraid to go to sleep. Every night I avoided sleep by reading by candlelight until I was exhausted. The nights became as traumatic as the days.

Severe pains in my chest and back recurred so frequently that I convinced myself that I was dying. I was at an age where dying was a terrifying thought—so much so that when I saw the local paper lying on the kitchen table, I avoided looking directly at it in case it was carelessly left open on the obituary page. There is irony in the fact that now I am obviously much closer to death than I was then, I never, to the amusement of my family, miss reading the obituaries.

One Sunday, the pain in my chest was so intense that I could barely walk the mile and a half to the church. On arrival, I slumped down in the church porch. The vicar's wife, Mrs. Phillips, looked at me closely and, with obvious concern, asked,

"Are you sure you are alright, Rosie?—you look so pale." Those words convinced me, without a shadow of doubt, that I was surely not long for this world.

After the service, I crept out of the churchyard trying to avoid looking at the gravestones—a stark reminder of what I was sure was shortly in store for me.

Mrs. Phillips sent a message to my grandmother to say that she should immediately call the doctor which frightened me even more but, of course, the examination revealed nothing. Psychological damage was not a consideration. Had it been, why should I, growing up in what to the outside world appeared to be a normal, loving home be suffering psychological trauma? We had become experts at burying the refuse of our lives underground where it was invisible to the world but would never fully decompose.

Haydn and I were fortunate, to an extent, that we could rely on each other for support which certainly helped us to maintain some degree of sanity. On the surface, Haydn refused to take our grandmother seriously, and he developed the nerve to stand up to her which none of her children ever had, even as adults. He saw, and helped me to see humour in the situation, and now, on the rare occasions that we get together, we can still laugh until the tears flow as we relive those days and reminisce over the bizarre antics of our grandmother.

Haydn tends to remember, also, the positive experiences, and there were good times, I must admit.

When we were ill, though rarely, my grandmother sent us to bed and looked after us like a real mother, bringing us all our meals, along with glasses of Lucozade and calling the doctor even at times when it may not have been necessary. She had grown up in an age where, before the discovery of penicillin, she had watched a child of her own die as well as those of neighbours. Illnesses of any kind were, therefore, taken very seriously.

I recall, when Haydn contracted measles he was kept in a darkened room, and I was made to sit in the room with him until I caught the disease. I don't think either of us felt at all sick, but I well remember how we enjoyed such rare pampering and how we looked forward to the days that Aunt Phyllis came home from the Mansion to read our favourite poems.

While she had no qualms about wringing a chicken's neck and feathering it for dinner, my grandmother always demonstrated kindness towards any of the farm animals that might be suffering. I well remember the day that one of the pullets had eaten so much corn that her crop was blocked. Without hesitation, and the skill of a surgeon, my grandmother cut open the chicken's crop, removed the corn and deftly sewed up the wound with a darning needle and thread while we watched in fascination and Aunt Blodwen, a nurse, almost fainted away. The chicken made a rapid and complete recovery. It took Aunt Blodwen much longer.

In the long winter evenings, it was necessary for us to make our own entertainment. My grandmother taught us to play card games:—Sevens, Whist, Strip-Jack-Naked. She taught us Whist well enough to participate in the village Whist Drives, and we felt important going along with her to play with the adults. Occasionally, she showed a modicum of pride in our skill.

We played cards or table skittles almost every evening except Sunday which was "The Lord's Day." There were times, though, when it suited my grandmother, that Sunday wasn't off limits—those were the days when she felt powerful enough to override even God.

Predictably, like a child, she didn't like to lose, so even at family times such as those, we could never relax. In a jiffy, she might have an out and out tantrum, and the cards would be thrown across the room. One night, in a terrible rage, she threw the whole pack onto the fire. The next morning, I remember seeing the charred remains of clubs, diamonds, spades and hearts lying amongst the ashes. My mind could not escape the symbolism in that picture.

Yes, there were good times as Haydn still reminds me, and we can now enjoy a good laugh together, but her unpredictable behaviour completely diminished her family's spirit through two generations.

While nightmares do grow paler in one's memory and pain gets washed away, only understanding, forgiveness and above all, humour can put one back on solid ground. I must thank Haydn for putting me there.

CHAPTER SEVEN

"If country life be healthful to the body it is no less so to the mind."
Ruffini

To my readers, it may seem somewhat paradoxical, therefore, for me to say that many of my memories of early childhood are happy ones. Perhaps, as Marcel Proust says, "'Remembrance of things past is not necessarily remembrance of things as they were." but when I reflect on my life, the powerful memories of a free and almost feral life in the countryside are now lodged uppermost in my mind.

Once we had escaped the war zone, we were connected to nature, released into beauty and tranquillity, free to roam in our vast outdoor playground, answerable to nothing and to no one. There, for days on end, we occupied ourselves in the fields and woods, constructing forts, damming streams, climbing trees, wading in ponds, collecting frogspawn, playing hide-and-seek in the hay and straw in the barns, under the hayricks and in the bracken that seemed to grow tall enough to blot out the sky. We became experts at recognizing the call of the birds, knew where they built their nests and the colour and size of their eggs.

Unwillingly, we came home, often soaking wet and mud splattered when we were called for meals. Our imagination was boundless, boredom never entered our lives.

Haydn loved to build things and I was always there by his side to be his helper. We built buggies from old farm machinery, wagon wheels and bits of metal that we found around the farm. One luxury model, built from an old pram chassis topped by a metal trunk, was our pride and joy. As the youngest, and the most gullible, I was always the one who had to test out the performance of the latest model.

That model, as it turned out, had a very short existence. Haydn persuaded me to sit in it at the top of a hill and then he let go. The buggy careened down the lane, took the corner at speed and hit a bank, throwing me six feet into the air. I wasn't too badly hurt, but the prized buggy was no more—the wheels were buckled beyond repair and the old, tin trunk bent out of shape. We sat together on the bank, for a long time, mourning our loss, and then we walked home, sadly, dragging the remains of the buggy.

At weekends, we wandered further afield, scrumped fruit from neighbouring orchards, investigated ruins of barns and tumbledown houses, picked arms full of wild daffodils, bluebells or foxgloves and returned home dragging a collection of useless treasures. My grandmother called us "guttersnipes." Aunt Phyllis always told us we were "brown as berries" and called me "Gypsy Meg," a reference to John Keats's poem—Meg Merrilies.

Like Meg Merrilies, our lives were spent mainly out of doors, but on Sundays, we took advantage of my grandmother's regular Sunday afternoon nap and tuned into the radio which was otherwise off limits to us.

When I was nine years old a new programme had started on the B.B.C. Light Programme called, "Educating Archie" featuring Peter Brough and his puppet, Archie Andrews. It is still one of those unsolvable mysteries how a ventriloquist and his dummy could appeal to a radio audience of 15 million, for eight years.

So many British actors and comedians, including Julie Andrews as Archie's girlfriend, made their start on that programme, and the catch phrases that were introduced are lodged for ever in the tiny brains and childish minds of my male British contemporaries who still giggle when they hear phrases such as, "jolly hockey sticks," "as the Art mistress said to the gardener," and

"I've arrived and to prove it I'm here."

We were always taught that people who lived in "Iron Curtain" countries were brainwashed, little realizing that we were, too, in a sophisticated B.B.C. way.

Immediately following the programme, the neighbourhood children always gathered at the farm, all arriving on their bicycles to play rounders or cricket. Haydn had been given a real cricket bat of which he was intensely proud, but our wickets were all crudely fashioned from bits of wood.

Those games continued, noisily and competitively until the last glimmer of light forced us inside, or earlier if our one and only cricket ball accidentally got hit into the garden and my grandmother, rising from her nap and ending our short respite, refused to let us retrieve it:

"Why should I have to put up with that bloody riff-raff tromping all over my flowers?"

We spent hours with Mrs. Murphy, an old and fascinating gypsy, dressed in authentic colourful clothing who came, every summer, to park her gypsy caravan on the other side of our garden hedge. Being Irish, she inhabited a world of fairies and leprechauns.

Her stories were gripping and for us, at the time, believable. How often, we made her repeat the one about her son, Tom, finding his way home through the dense fog with the help of a goblin sitting on his head. In vain we looked for goblins.

The Bradley children, who lived across the fields from us, were our constant companions and partners in crime. My grandmother told us that the Bradleys were "the scum of the earth," but I knew that the scum did not come much thicker or closer to the surface than in the Jones family. While the British class system leads everyone to believe that they are that much better than the next person, it was, and still is, a constant source of amazement to me that my grandmother could believe that she was further up the totem pole of life than any of our neighbours. She constantly referred to the "lower-classes." I wondered just how low one could go?

Hazel Bradley was the eldest, and just my age, so became my bosom friend and ally until we were separated by the ill-conceived wisdom of the British education system.

She was tall and pretty with long blond hair that she wore in neat plaits. I was jealous of her naturally wavy hair. Mine was so straight that I could never keep the ribbons in. One plait was always undone and the ribbon caught up on a hedge or a barbed-wire fence.

I lost so many ribbons that my grandmother decided that my hair should be cut short, much against my will. Aunt Phyllis was ordered to do the dreadful deed, a lack of skill not being considered a hindrance. She put a basin on my head and cut around the edge. The outcome was about as good as the cut she gave my grandfather which resulted in him being too embarrassed to remove his hat in public for six weeks.

Hazel and her younger sisters were the only girls I knew who wore shorts, which seemed far more practical than the cotton dresses that I wore along with my Wellington boots, but my grandmother considered shorts to be the height of indecency:

"Can you credit it?—that woman lettin' those girls run around like that with their asses showin'? They may as well 'ave bugger all on if you ask me. Mark my words, she's asking for trouble an' no mistake."

Hazel's younger brother, Tony, professed to be in love with me for most of my childhood. He sent love letters, bunches of wildflowers and sweets through his sisters or Haydn, and he claimed that he was going to marry me when we grew up. I thought of him just as a good friend, never taking him seriously. At times, his constant attention annoyed me, and I was less than gracious. Perhaps, without realizing it, I broke his heart.

Mrs. Bradley was a very motherly type whose home was always open to the waifs and strays of the neighbourhood. That is how, I am sure, she thought of us. It was a complete shambles, like most of the homes in the country, but filled with love and laughter. She organized great birthday parties for her seven children to which we were always invited and a wonderful Guy Fawkes party on the fifth of November every year, with a massive bonfire, on which to burn the Guy—an effigy of straw stuffed into my grandfather's old shirt and dungarees—that could be seen for miles around. She was aware that in our house birthdays were no cause for celebration and parties of any kind were frowned upon. I suspect that Mrs. Bradley knew more about our bizarre lives than we thought she did.

Mr. Bradley—"That ol' Walter Bradley," to use my grandmother's terminology for the gentleman of the house, was a very friendly, jolly individual who made gallons of cider from the cider apples in his orchard, most of which he drank himself; it was both the cause of his jolliness and his untimely death from cirrhosis of the liver. Mrs. Bradley was left to run a farm and to raise her seven children alone. I remember my grandmother's sympathetic comment on the day of the funeral:

"Good riddance to the likes of 'im, I say—she'll be a lot better off without that drunken ol' sot. 'e should've bin castrated years ago."

She did not spell that out, but I knew about castration as I had watched my grandfather castrating the male yearling sheep with a vicious looking instrument which, when not in use, hung menacingly behind the pantry door. Castration, it seemed, to me, would have been an unnecessarily harsh treatment for "ol' Walter."

The Bradley's farm was a real farm with huge barns and sheds. We spent so much time there playing in the great hay lofts, daring each other to leap onto beds of hay and straw on the barn floor below. It was a miracle that there were never any broken limbs. Perhaps it was because of a lack of adult supervision that we learned how to take care of ourselves and were allowed to judge our own limitations.

Our games only took a lewd turn if the notorious Dai Thomas came along. He was the boy who introduced the show-and-tell games. In one, I recall, the girls were dared to stand on their heads against the hayrick to show their knickers—a game in which the Bradley girls had a distinct advantage. Obviously, we were not unwilling participants. That, however, was about the limit of our advance towards sexual depravity.

Like other children growing up, we played nasty tricks on people that seemed so amusing to us at the time. On our way home from school, we passed by a hut where old Joe Penry lived. It was one of those huts that had been left over from the stage-coach days so it had a metal roof. We couldn't pass by without throwing rocks at the roof until old Joe came out to chase us and call us every name under the sun.

That was a puerile act like most of our pranks, but one that was much more serious was when Haydn and I thought that it would be fun to lock Mrs. Murphy into her gypsy caravan for the night. We were quite old enough to understand the consequences if she had been taken ill or the caravan had burst into flames.

The next morning, when my grandmother heard Mrs. Murphy banging on the inside of her door and screaming to be let out, we knew we were in trouble. The beating we got that day was well deserved.

Wales always receives more than its share of rain, but, throughout my childhood, I only recall clear blue skies, long, hot, dry summers and snowy winters.

The winter of 1946-1947 was memorable for the sheer depth of snow. I remember the wonderful peaceful silence as that deep, white blanket of snow enveloped the earth. In Wales, we were cut off from the outside world for days on end which, to a small child, was so exciting, but how was it that a whole country could be so negatively affected by something so magical?

A shortage of coal caused the power stations to shut down, and the government of the day brought in measures to cut electricity consumption—not of any concern to those, like us, who had none. Radio broadcasts were limited and television services suspended but, again, meaningless to a family who had never had television. Public morale was, apparently, so low that people turned on the government and the Minister of Fuel and Power received death threats which resulted in him having to be put under police guard. By the sound of it, those were not quite, "the good old days" of which we are constantly reminded.

The only immediate concern on the farm would have been for the animals and their food supply. The snow was too deep for the sheep to forage for grass, and many of them became trapped in the deep snow. Across the country, many animals were lost, but my grandfather was proud that, through his efforts, all of ours were saved.

There were other years, too, when the snow drifts were so deep that it would be several days before the postman and the tradespeople could get through to the rural areas. With school inaccessible, those were halcyon days for us.

The Bradleys had a very steep field that was perfect for sledding. All our sleds were homemade, but the most ingenious and the fastest one was made by Haydn from a long sheet of galvanized roofing tin with the front end curved up. Eight or more of us could sit on it at once which made it move at breakneck speed. If we had fallen on its lethal edges, we could easily have severed a limb, but we were oblivious to the danger, and there was never any parental concern. We would stay out all day long until our clothes were soaked through and our hands and feet were cold to the point of frostbite. How painful a process it was to restore the circulation!

It was not all play though. We were expected to help on the farm in any way we could, but I did not consider it work.

In the winter, we gathered and sawed wood for the fire. I loved the squeak and the push and pull rhythm of the saw as it cut through the wood. There was something so soothing about the repetitive movement. I loved to stack the cut logs neatly and watch the pile grow taller in the woodshed. Thanks to Haydn's perseverance, I was a dab hand at the cross-cut saw by the age of seven and knowledgeable about various kinds of wood because of the ease or difficulty of sawing. We loved to saw birch because it was as soft as butter, but beech and oak were so much harder and, therefore, required greater effort.

We had rented pasture some way from the house and it was our job, also, to take the cows and sheep to graze and bring them back in the evening. One day, one of the cows was grazing too close to the hedge of a neighbour, Nellie Powell. Nellie and her husband Elijah leapt out, shouting and threatening us and in the altercation which followed, Nellie had the audacity to kick one of our cows. That put an end to our relationship with Nellie and Elijah for once and for all. We were never allowed to speak to them again. My grandmother was not big on forgiveness:

"'ow dare she, that 'ol bitch. If I'd bin there, I'd 've kicked 'er right up the ass."

Haydn taught me how to catch animals that were considered pests. There was no time for sentimentality towards wild animals in the country, and perhaps it was an early form of censorship, rather than a coincidence, that there were no Beatrix Potter books in our small collection.

I wonder at my ruthlessness and cruelty—how I was so easily coerced into believing that rabbits and moles were vermin and needed to be got rid of in the most barbaric of ways.

I am also amazed how we could so readily compartmentalize our emotions. Animals that served our need—the cats which controlled the rodents and the dogs that rounded up the sheep were our pets and therefore treated with love and respect. Losing a favourite pet was always heart-breaking. How often, we performed a burial service, made a moss covered grave, soaked it with our tears, and erected a crude wooden cross with the letters R.I.P.

Haydn showed me how to set the snares in the rabbit runs and metal traps underground in the mole tunnels. I would share in his pride when we had caught a rabbit by its neck or squished a mole in a metal trap. The day we set a new kind of trap that had a spring at either end and caught two moles at once, we were ecstatic. How could I have had no feeling for those cute little creatures? I have been filled with remorse since and while looking up suitable quotes on the futility of such an emotion was encouraged by this one:

"Things without all remedy should be without regard. What's done is done." until I realized that the words were those of Lady Macbeth.

One of our biggest treats was to go rabbiting with my grandfather. That was a Sunday morning ritual when we caught enough rabbits to eat during the week and for my grandmother to take to market. We would carry a hammer, the nets and pegs while my grandfather would hang on grimly to the vicious ferret scrambling and fighting in a sack. He would carefully put the nets over all the holes in the rabbit warren and then, holding it by the scruff of the neck to avoid being bitten, put the ferret down a hole to flush out the rabbits. When they hurtled in fear into the nets, he would remove them from the netting, bash them over the head with the hammer and throw them on the ground. In this way, we would amass ten or twelve in a morning. Their limp, lifeless, bodies, eyes bulging, would be hung by slit feet onto a long pole which Haydn and I would carry proudly home.

My grandmother would splay the blood-splattered corpses along the railings, split them open, remove the putrid smelling guts—delicacies for the dogs and cats—and skin them ready for market, saving one or two for rabbit stew.

That practice ended abruptly when myxomatosis arrived. The sight of those hapless creatures, with their bulging heads and blinded eyes, bumping their way around the countryside dampened any desire for rabbit stew.

The rabbits have now returned almost threefold, and, with stronger genetic immunity, have become, once again, a plague. It seems the more we tamper with nature, the more problems we create. Spike Milligan, comedian and creator of quirky little verses said it best:

"A baby rabbit
With eyes full of pus,
This is the work
Of scientific us."

In my advancing years, I have atoned for my murderous past. Many pests in my garden are grateful, including the slugs which, every morning, get picked up gently and taken for long relocation walks.

I feel a little hypocritical when I rail at those who destroy them ruthlessly by poisoning them with bait, chopping them to pieces or drowning them in beer. I've even heard of one person who chewed them up in the garburator—that's what may be called an insinkerator or a rubbish disposal unit in Wales, although I doubt that many people own them. When I investigated their popularity in Great Britain—what is a common household appliance in Canada—I came upon a comment from a person who thought "they had an air of upscale suburban luxury." "My word! Haven't I come a long way since my childhood in Wales?" I thought.

I probably wouldn't have the stomach for it now, but I revelled in cleaning out the hen houses and the cowsheds—shovelling out the dung, washing down the floor with buckets of clean water from the tank beside the shed and putting down fresh, sweet smelling straw for the chickens, ducks and cows.

Carrying water from the well was almost a full-time job. With the endless cups of tea that were drunk, a bucket did not go far. When Haydn and I went together, there was more chance of a full bucket making it home. When the well ran dry, which happened almost every summer, we would have to walk a mile or more down the lane and along a path through the woods to a spring that never dried up. The path was dark and eerie and, in my imagination, was the one where Little Red Riding Hood had met the wolf. We trod very warily down that path.

The seasons were marked by the farming year: the lambing season, sheep washing, dipping and shearing, grass mowing and harvest time. We were involved in them all.

Before mechanization, the hay had to be scythed, raked and turned by hand. I remember so well the sweet smell of sun dried hay mixed with the meadow flowers— so pungent that it hurt our noses as we forked it up to make a hayrick in the corner of the field.

Lambing time was a busy time for my grandfather. He would often be up at night to help a sheep that was having difficulty giving birth. Sometimes, he would have to seek the assistance of my grandmother who would come to the ewe's aid, delivering its baby with the skill of a midwife. When a sheep had twins, or occasionally triplets, any lambs rejected by their mother would be bottle fed and become our pets. Eventually, all the lambs would end up going to market and we accepted that as inevitable.

One very special pet lamb called Betsy lived alongside the dogs—the sheep dogs and my own cocker spaniel, Gyp, until she believed she was one. Like dogs, she developed a habit of chasing vehicles. Few passed our house, but she would patiently lie in wait for one and then gambol after it. Often, she would wait until one came back in the other direction and then hitch a lift home. She so endeared herself to everyone that she saved herself from market and lived out her life on the farm, becoming a mother herself many times over.

Every year, we raised a pig which was also our beloved pet until the day it was slaughtered, turned into pork and bacon, cured in salt and hung around the kitchen walls. The screams of that poor creature, while being stuck, upset me terribly as they reverberated around the farm—even louder than my grandmother's screams as she knifed herself under the stairs.

We always helped in the huge vegetable garden. Uncle Philip, when he occasionally came home to take a break from his other mysterious life, would set us tasks to do in his absence—carrying barrow-loads of composted dung from the dung heap—preparing a piece of ground for planting—thinning the young seedlings. On his return, he would inspect our work with a critical eye. He had exacting standards. He taught us well.

Indoors, we were responsible for separating the cream from the milk, churning the butter and making cheese, the taste of which had no similarity whatsoever to what we eat today. The back kitchen and the separator always smelled sickeningly of sour milk. There were no means of refrigeration and nothing ever got thoroughly washed, but we all grew up to be healthy despite, or perhaps because of the absence of the health authorities. We kept enough milk to drink in tea and the skimmed milk and butter milk was fed to the calves and the cats and dogs.

What was interesting, busy and even exciting for us, though, constituted a very hard life for my grandparents though I did not appreciate it at the time. Life on the farm, in the beauty and peace of the countryside was so often our salvation—for them, so often drudgery.

MEMOIR OF "A SLOPPY, SPINELESS, CREATURE"

CHAPTER EIGHT

"Use It Up, Wear It Out, Make It Do, Or Do Without!"
Caption from one of the posters encouraging frugality
during the years of rationing in WWII

Before the war, around 55 million tons of food were
imported to Britain, but when Germany began sinking
British merchant vessels with submarines and
battleships, it became necessary to implement a system
of rationing for food, clothing, furniture and fuel.

Food rationing began in January of 1940, four
months after the outbreak of war and almost two years
before I was born. It lasted for some things until 1954 by
which time I was thirteen years old.

I had no idea, while I was growing up, what
rationing meant for the majority of British citizens
because, on the farm, my family was well supplied with
meat, bacon, eggs, milk, butter, cheese and vegetables.
Everyone was issued a ration book with stamps that had
to be given to the grocer, butcher or baker in exchange
for a limited amount of goods, but we were able to
donate some of our stamps to people who were not so
fortunate.

The allowances were meagre for those who, unlike
us, had no ready supply. People were expected, for
example, to live on just one egg and three rashers of
bacon per week, while we could eat eggs and bacon
every day.

We had no need to go shopping for the few items
that we didn't produce, as everything was delivered right
to the door. The grocer brought us limited amounts of
tea, salt, flour, Mcvitie's digestive biscuits, Robertson's
marmalade and sugar.

I do remember being affected by the lack of sugar,
because every week, when our ration was delivered, my
grandmother divided it up into jam jars containing each

person's allowance with names clearly displayed on the outside of the jar—another hazardous practice in a turbulent household like ours; it caused a great deal of haggling, accusations that someone had sneaked a teaspoon of sugar from another person's jar, and resulted in more than a few fist fights.

I also remember that one package of Digestive biscuits did not go far in a family of six or seven. That wasn't such a hardship, though, as my grandmother regularly filled our stomachs with Welsh cakes—she called them bakestones—and rock cakes—both very aptly named. My grandfather was the unlucky recipient of more than a few of those.

McVitie's Digestive biscuits are a prominent feature in British culture and still feature in my life. We are never without a fresh roll of them. The first thing my grandchildren do, when they visit, is to dive into the cupboard in search of them. A friend of mine, Chris, has a prized, retro, metal canister which holds a complete roll—she's probably not aware that it would fetch a small fortune on E-Bay—which has accompanied us on all our walking and cycling trips together. In our opinion, there's nothing quite so comforting as a nice cup of tea with a Digestive, and it is still the most popular biscuit for dunking.

Few people know that the Digestive biscuit was McVitie and Price's first major biscuit, and, it is claimed, it was created in 1892 by a new young employee, Alexander Grant, who went on to be head of the company. An earlier biscuit had been made by two Scottish doctors in 1839 because they believed that the high baking soda content was good for digestion.

The Chocolate Digestive was created in 1925 and for those readers who love trivia, they may be interested to know that 71 million packages of those get eaten in the U.K. every year. That's 52 biscuits per second, so it's no wonder the British, in general, have such dreadful teeth.

Another interesting titbit is that McVitie made the wedding cake of Princess Elizabeth and Sir Philip Mountbatten, and in 2011, Prince William chose a groom's cake made from 1,700 McVitie's Rich Tea biscuits and 17 kilograms of chocolate.

Robertson's marmalade also has a fascinating history. During the war, and for years afterwards, it came with little paper golliwogs at the top of the jar. Many children received enamel brooches and badges after they had collected a certain number of paper ones, but we didn't seem to eat enough marmalade to qualify.

John Robertson may have got his idea of the golliwog from a lady named Florence Kate Upton who began writing children's books about a character called "Golliwogg" in 1895. As she did not patent the name, John Robertson changed it to "Golliwog" in 1910, and it became the company's mascot until 2002 when it was jettisoned because of racial connotations. Little did Florence Kate Upton realize that a hundred years after she had created her lovable little character that it would be reviled as racist. The Brits are still not known for political correctness, but golliwogs, I am happy to say, have become a thing of the past.

But, returning to the subject of rationing, I did not really know, until many years later, just how long it had lasted. Clothing was rationed until 1949 and petrol until 1950. Soap was also rationed until 1950, but its absence probably had not made any noticeable difference to the bathing habits of my family.

It wasn't until 1954 that all food rationing ended, but I believe that there isn't an old person living today who doesn't remember the actual day, in 1953, that sweets finally came off rationing. All children over the age of five years had been allotted a small quantity throughout the war years, but suddenly, overnight, they could buy sweets to their heart's content—more than enough to rot all their teeth for just a few pennies. I was twelve years old but remember that day as if it was yesterday.

Today, with such abundance and choice, consumers might wonder about the possible hardship of rationing. In truth, 60% of the population were very much in favour of it, and almost everyone did their part to conserve and share.

Citizens were encouraged to keep bees and to grow vegetables on their own plots as well as in public spaces. They were called Victory gardens and there were so many posters encouraging the practice— advertisements with quirky little drawings imploring people to "Sow seeds for Victory" and "Dig on for Victory." Posters encouraging the conservation of food proliferated: Food Is a Weapon. Don't Waste It! Can All You Can! Know All Your Onions. Make the Food Go All the Way! and, We Can Do It! depicting a strong-armed woman flaunting bulging biceps that rivalled Popeye's.

Even the recycling of bones was encouraged, to be boiled down to make glue, ground up for fertilizer or made into glycerine for explosive for shells and bombs. It was claimed that a single chop bone weighing 2 oz. could supply the explosive charge for two rounds of ammunition for R.A.F. Hurricane fighter guns.

Of course, there were people who felt deprived, and there were the cheats who managed to acquire more than their fair share. A black market soon developed. There are always those who find ways to circumvent the system.

I have a vivid memory of my uncle Philip turning up on leave in possession of a large tin of Cadbury's chocolate fingers. No one knew the source or asked, but my grandmother, true to form, had to offer her usual wisdom on her son's character:

"It's just like 'im to be up to some jiggery-pokery. 'es as cunnin' as a shite'ouse rat."

It didn't, however, stop her from diving straight into

the spoils.

Those long years of rationing taught us a lesson that can never be forgotten by my generation. Following the war, so many of us have benefited from the boom times that eventually followed, but, as fortunate as we have been, most of us still live our lives according to the age-old proverb, "Waste Not, Want Not."

The family at Oakdale—in our hand-me-downs—my grandmother and I in Wellingtons. Left to right—Haydn, Lewis, (Marion's husband), Blodwen, me, Phyllis, Yvonne, (her eldest daughter), Irene and my grandmother

CHAPTER NINE

"I just thank God that I didn't grow up with so much money or privilege because you had to create ways to make it happen."
Kim Basinger

That sentiment didn't only apply to country children growing up with little, but to adults too, and while I may have given the impression that my grandparents' life was one continuous slog, they were always able to find a little time and money to purchase the odd little treat and create a simple social life for themselves.

Much of their entertainment revolved around the church—whist drives, beetle drives, musical evenings, tea parties—until the Mansion, which housed the young men returning from the war, became the social hub of the district. Not only did the Mansion provide a social life but it also provided employment for my mother and her sisters, a source of men friends and, eventually, for some, a husband.

I gained no less than three uncles from the Mansion, including Uncle "Ginge"—another of the "shite'ouse rat" persuasion—who married Aunt Maisie in secret, after she had absconded to become a bus conductress. That marriage was particularly unpopular with my grandmother:

"What in 'ell's name would make 'er run off with that rotter? 'e's nothin' but the scum of the earth. She needs 'er 'ead read an' no mistake."

Immediately after the marriage, to which none of the family were invited, my mother and I were surprised to meet Maisie pushing a pram down the street in Monmouth. She had not informed anyone in the family that she was expecting a happy event. She had, in fact, adopted a baby boy, Paul. There was much speculation as to the origin of the baby, but my grandmother was convinced that it had to be the offspring of one of Ginge's "whores," and she stated so with great authority and frequency.

There were other men from the Mansion who were not quite so successful in their quest for marital bliss. They were very popular with Haydn and me because they showered us with half-crowns, to gain favour with my mother and my aunts. One of them, we later read about in the Sunday paper—The *News of the World*. He had been caught stealing ladies' knickers off washing lines throughout South Wales. Could it have been his traumatic war experiences or rejection by my aunt Marion that had caused him to go careering off the rails? She would accept no responsibility.

There were frequent dances and social evenings at the Mansion where everyone was wildly enthusiastic about "The Jitterbug"—a kind of swing dance that was popular at the time. After the departure of the American troops, following D-Day, English couples were being warned not to continue doing energetic "rude American dancing," but by 1946, it was a craze in Britain, and the Welsh country folk embraced it with a passion.

Music and dancing played such an important part in the lives of the soldiers fighting overseas as well as those on the home front. Songs that were popular during WWII are woven so deeply into my core; when I hear the music of Glenn Miller and particularly the voice of Vera Lynn, I am filled with such nostalgia for those evenings when neighbours came together in friendship and joy, at such a horrific time.

Vera Lynn became known as "The Forces Sweetheart" and her songs are still bringing tears to the eyes of those who fought in or lived through the war, as she approaches her one hundredth birthday. We owe so much to her and all the performers who entertained the troops and boosted morale at home and abroad.

At the Mansion, we made friends with all the young

men as well as the few former prisoners-of-war who did not return to their homeland immediately after the war was over.

They were always kind to us, and we were fascinated by their strange way of speaking. Perhaps some of them had wives and children back in Germany. Others stayed on to marry local girls—just one more scandal in the eyes of our grandmother:

"Good God almighty!—if she 'asn't upped an' got 'erself in the family way with one of those bloody ol' Germans. What in 'ell's name is the bloody world comin' to?"

We also, on occasion, went to "the pictures" as a family and, if money allowed, enjoyed a cup of tea and a cream bun prior to the film.

You could enter the cinema at any time during the performance and keep watching until you came back to the part where you came in. If you were enjoying the film, or if it wasn't time to catch your bus, you could watch it all the way through again several times. This meant that there were always people arriving and departing and blocking the view.

Smoking was permitted so, as time went on, a dense pall of smoke descended slowly from the ceiling until you were enshrouded in a London-style smog; your eyes began to smart, as the characters on the screen gradually faded from view.

As the film ended, and the credits began to appear, we knew that we had to make our escape before the first Grip's name came up, or we would be trapped. Whispers would be heard throughout the cinema:

"Quick, let's get out before the King," and there would be a mad scramble for the doors, as people risked life and limb just to avoid standing for the playing of "God Save the King," the custom following every performance in those days. If you hadn't managed to make it to the door, you were expected to stand rigidly to attention, until it was over, so speed was of the essence.

It was cheap entertainment—only nine pence—about 20 cents, to sit in the front seats, so if you could live with a distorted picture, a crick in the neck and hair and clothing that stunk for the rest of the week, it was an absolute bargain.

Most of the films, however, were quite unsuitable for small children, but, in any case, I would usually drift off to sleep and have to be carried out at the end.

One film that I do remember, though, because it was so disturbing and probably coincided with my period of intense fear of death, was Hamlet, starring Laurence (later Lord) Olivier. It was released in 1948. I would have been only seven years old at the time.

Most Saturday afternoons, though, my mother and Aunt Maisie would go to Monmouth alone. They would spend most of the morning preparing themselves for the outing, primping and preening, daubing themselves with cheap perfume—Evening in Paris, which came in a dark blue bottle—making themselves up like my teacher, Mrs. Powell.

A great deal of time was apportioned to the preparation of the legs in those days. Nylons were unavailable, unless, of course, one had had the good fortune to have met up with an American, rather than a drunken Irishman. My mother and her sisters tanned their legs with a cream that was made especially for the purpose, or, if they couldn't afford it, they used gravy browning—not the best option as there was more than one case of a woman attracting a large pack of dogs that she could not manage to shake off.

Having applied the brown colouring, my mother and aunt would then, painstakingly, draw a black line down the back of the legs to give the appearance of nylons.

All this preparation was probably to meet young men. Had my grandmother known what they were up to, she would have called them whores.

While we were friendly enough with the neighbours, except for Nellie and Elijah following the cow kicking episode, there was very little visiting or entertaining within our home. Other than the would-be suitors from the Mansion, I only remember one or two neighbours ever coming to the house.

One of those characters was Albert Llewellyn, a tramp like old gentleman who made a point of coming once a month to have a cup of tea with my grandmother to talk about memorable thunderstorms and the unusual number of tragedies that had occurred in the neighbourhood over the years.

It was true that there was hardly a home that had not been affected in some way. Our home was the scene of an ongoing tragedy which was unknown outside of our four walls and, therefore, not a topic for discussion. Conversation always revolved around those who had suffered a painful or sudden death of some kind: Several farmers had committed suicide or been killed by an overturning tractor, Mr. Jones, next door, had been crushed by a steam-roller, and, as cars became more common, many people had been involved in head-on collisions on the narrow lanes. Ernie Morgan had died in a crash on his way home from Barry Island, a child had been smothered in mud when a gate fell on top of him, and another had died from eating poisonous berries.

These stories were repeated with relish, in true Welsh fashion, over and over again. The Welsh have such a morbid fascination with death and dying—the gorier the death, the better. It was clearly both my grandmother's and Albert's belief, though, that some supernatural force was at play. There was even talk that 'Ol Robinson' was perhaps responsible. My grandmother also believed that tragedy had struck those who had allowed their visitors to come in through one door of the house and leave through another, a superstition that I'm almost embarrassed to say, still holds me firmly in its grip.

The whole village was in mourning after Sheila Hale, the girl who had been bitten by the adder in childhood, drowned herself and her two young children in a water-butt. Returning to the barn with the cows for milking, her husband saw the water slopping over the edge of the water-butt and knew instinctively, the horror that awaited him. Sheila had been an unfortunate victim of postnatal depression, but my grandmother, of course, was convinced that her assessment of Sheila's mental state following the snake bite had been correct all along:

"That girl was never right in the 'ead after that adder got 'er."

My grandmother always revelled in the discussions with Albert, but, at the same time, she dreaded the visits because he had not washed himself or his clothing for many a year and, besides that, he had a severe bladder problem—his smell preceded him like an early warning system and permeated the lanes for hours after he had passed by. Nevertheless, his visits were an essential part of my grandmother's social life so, mostly, she managed to put up with him.

On occasion, however, she felt that she just wasn't up to facing him, so we would be sent to tell him that she wasn't home. One day, when she spied him ambling up the path, she decided to hide outside in the motor-house yard, while I was forced to go to the door to lie to him.

Albert was having none of it. He pushed his way into the house and took up his usual position in the kitchen, expecting his customary cup of tea. He was in no hurry to leave, so while I listened to the stories of the tragedies and terrifying thunderstorms that had occurred throughout his life, my grandmother spent several hours hiding outside, her anger building to a crescendo.

Eventually, I managed to get rid of old Albert, but by that time, my grandmother was so livid that she threatened to kill me. Scurrying into the kitchen and grabbing the carving knife, she rammed the table up to the piano to trap me, but I was fast and managed to clamber out under the table. Haydn, not having the sense to keep his mouth shut, dared to point out that she had brought the situation upon herself. Fortunately, Albert was also deaf, otherwise he would have heard our terrified screams as she chased us into the woods, brandishing the knife, bellowing,

"I should've listened to 'em when they told me not to take you little buggers in. I should've let the pair of you rot in 'ell. Don't bother to come back 'ere. Go back to that bloody drunken scum where you belong."

Albert, oblivious to the unfolding drama, tootled aimlessly back up the lane, leaving his urinary perfume hanging heavily on the air.

MEMOIR OF "A SLOPPY, SPINELESS, CREATURE"

CHAPTER TEN

"Change can be good, but it's always tough to let go of the past."
Emily Giffi

It was a huge change for me when I was taken away from Tregare School against my will. I had been one in a class of four in a school of eleven students in my protected, narrow world. Now I was expected to strike out into new territory. I was apprehensive about what awaited me.

Haydn was thirteen, so left Tregare school at the same time to attend the Secondary Modern School. There was no more dawdling; we suddenly had time restraints. The bus left from Marble Hall some way beyond the school, so until I owned my first bicycle at the age of twelve, we walked or ran along with the Bradleys who were already conversant with life beyond Tregare.

My first day at Overmonnow Girls' School was painful. The headmistress, filling out my registration information, called me in to ask me the name of my father. One cannot underestimate how traumatic divorce is for small children. In the nineteen forties when it was virtually unheard of, it was more so for me. I felt ashamed. I felt responsible. It affected my self-esteem. It was a load I bore every day of my life. I was too embarrassed to tell the awful truth, so I pretended that I didn't know my father's name. The headmistress thought this to be unusual and, as I squirmed on the chair and wrung my hands in front of her desk, she continued to question me, even bringing in another teacher who badgered me to the point of tears, and showed her impatience by demanding,

"Well, for goodness sake, what do your mother and your granny call him?" I knew that wasn't the answer she was looking for and, had I given it, my presence at my new school may have been very short-lived. Needless to say, I felt so distressed being put in that awkward situation. Again, I remembered my recurring dream. Things had got off to a dismal start.

In a class of 25 to 30 students, I was put into the capable hands of Miss Kathleen Price. She was a brittle woman who appeared to live on a diet of apples. She was deathly pale and thin to the point of anorexia, had thin mousy hair and a thin face as well as a thin tolerance for bad behaviour. She never cracked a smile.

Her only goal in life was to get as many of her pupils as possible through the Eleven-Plus exam. This she did by ridicule and bullying. Having the advantage of being well versed in that kind of treatment, I thrived on her methods.

Many of the students were more worldly town children, but there were the poorer children from the council estates who my grandmother called, "that bunch of ruffians." A ruffian was exactly what I had been brought up to be, and country children, being so strong, always had the upper hand in any gang warfare that occurred.

As we waited for the bus after school, and those "ruffians" made their way home, a fight would break out on the street. We loved every minute of those battles with sticks and rocks flying, hair pulling, punching and kicking. I would often arrive home with my clothes covered in mud and ripped to shreds, and there would be hell to pay, as well as a strong reprimand from Miss Price and the school headmistress the following morning, but as hardened little hooligans, the warnings didn't stop us. I had an advantage—I had grown up on a battlefield—I wanted to fight. I saw it as a legitimate outlet for my anger at the world.

Once I had buried my initial humiliation, I enjoyed my new school. The educational methods were far more rigorous and gardening did not feature at all in the curriculum, but there were so many more activities in which I could participate.

I revelled in the track and field practices which prepared us for Sports Day. We were divided into houses to encourage intense competition. I was athletic and excelled in all the events.

At Overmonnow's Girls' School—aged 10 years

Parents were rarely seen at schools during my childhood, but Sports Day was an exception. What a sight!—there they sat in their deck chairs, lining the edge of the field, eating their soggy tomato sandwiches, pouring cups of tea from their thermos flasks, their heads protected from the sun by knotted handkerchiefs.

Country dancing was a big part of our lives. Miss Price prepared us for demonstrations and competitions at country shows and fairs. Her dedication resulted in our enthusiastic reception and frequent successes.

It was during the time that I was at Overmonnow Girls' School that King George died on the sixth of February 1952. The whole country went into mourning. Britain was still recovering from the effects of six years of war. It was a further blow which seemed to send the country into a downward spiral. Britain had hosted what was known as the Austerity Olympics in 1948 and the Festival of Britain in 1951, but those two events, of which I was largely unaware, had not resulted in the country's renewed buoyancy.

The Korean War had been going on for almost two years—more than 60 years later, North and South Korea seem no closer to a peaceful solution—but I had never really taken any interest in world affairs until the King's death. I began listening to every news bulletin on the B.B.C. Home Service. Death was an event. An English king's death was a major event.

The following year, the mood of the country was boosted greatly by the Coronation of Queen Elizabeth II on the second of June. That was the first time that I saw television.

I was eleven years old. We were invited to a home in the town to watch the ceremony—thirty-five of us gathered around the family's twelve inch black and white set. All over Britain, tens of thousands of people were doing the same, and many, like me, were watching television—the "goggle box"—for the first time. The reception was so poor that we could hardly make out the Royals, but it was a very exciting moment in my life.

Those were celebratory times marked by street parties everywhere. Even at Oakdale, everyone got into the mood, decorating the outside of the house with strings of Union Jacks. A party was held in a field opposite Tregare church. There were races and games. My mother, as usual, won the ankle competition—the Welsh substitute for "Miss World." Every child received a commemorative Coronation mug. I have mine still. At school, a competition was held to produce the best scrap book of the Coronation. Always having had a flair for neatness and detail, I was not surprised to win.

Reverting to the subject of television, for a moment, so many of my generation will remember their first viewing only in connection with the Coronation, but few will recall, the following year, a B.B.C. adaptation of George Orwell's *Nineteen Eighty-Four* which had been published a few years earlier—an apocalyptic look at what the future might hold.

Alas! with the closest goggle box seven miles away in Monmouth, I couldn't watch it which was, as it turned out, just as well because it had a preliminary warning that it was "unsuitable for children and those with weak nerves."—much like the future life that Orwell predicted.

I spent two years under the tutelage of Miss Price. She was always hard on me which made me think that she disliked me. In reality, I think it was just a show of her determination to ensure that I would pass the Eleven-Plus.

The day that I was scheduled to sit the exam would have been just like any other day to me, but I recognized how important it must have been to my mother when I was bought new clothes for the occasion—a soft, warm, yellow and grey striped cardigan, and a scratchy grey, pleated skirt which, I remember, caused me discomfort throughout the exam.

The day that the results were announced, Hazel and I and all our friends had missed the school bus—not an infrequent occurrence—so I was not at school in time for any accolades that might have been bestowed. On arrival, we accepted the usual verbal abuse for being late and the common punishment—no dessert and five hundred lines to be written during the lunch break— but it was only an hour before the end of the day that Miss Price offhandedly mumbled, almost as if it pained her to say it,

"By the way, you won a scholarship to Monmouth School for Girls."

I don't remember feeling any sense of pride or elation, but that afternoon, I met Aunt Maisie in the street and casually told her that I had passed the exam. She was so thrilled that she gave me £1—the equivalent of $2.00—a small fortune to me.

Hazel's reaction was not so positive. Our relationship changed from that day. We had been separated into two distinct camps. In her eyes, she had become an eleven-year-old failure and I a winner. Only time would tell.

CHAPTER ELEVEN

"You can take the girl out of the country, but you can't take the country out of the girl."
Origin Unknown

I laugh heartily when my husband jokingly repeats this oft' used saying without realizing what an enormous challenge I must have created for the teachers of Monmouth School for Girls and how painful a process it was for me.

I had lived for so long in the shelter of Tregare, amongst people of my class, that I was completely unaware of how different I was from those in the outside world. At my new school, I was the proverbial square peg in a round hole.

Monmouth School for Girls

Monmouth School for Girls is an imposing institution, standing on a hill overlooking the town. It was first founded and established in 1614 by a local merchant haberdasher—William Jones—no known relation—and was built on its present site by the Worshipful Company of Haberdashers in 1897. On special occasions, such as Speech Days, the members would arrive with great pomp and ceremony, decked out in their blue ermine trimmed robes in a scene from another century.

You may well ask what a haberdasher is, and what exactly is worshipful about him. The Oxford dictionary defines haberdasher as, "a dealer in small articles of dress," and worshipful is one of those archaic British words given to groups or societies which, presumably, were worthy of being worshipped.

Monmouth School for Girls had become a direct grant grammar school in 1946 under the Education Act of 1944 and, as a grant aided establishment, was forced to take in a number of students who passed the Eleven-Plus exam. The rest of the students were fee-paying or scholarship winners from middle and upper-class homes in other parts of the country. They were full-time or weekly boarders. The school has since become wholly independent and is currently known as Haberdashers' Monmouth School for Girls.

The day students were already perceived to be distinctly lower-class and the likes of me, the Eleven-Plus riff-raff, in a subclass of our own.

While I was unaware of what was really in store for me at my new school, I revelled in all the brand-new uniform pieces that had to be bought for me, right down to the three pairs of navy blue bloomers with elasticated legs. I can still conjure up the warmth of the white viyella blouses, the stiffness of the gymslip and recall the new smell of the materials.

I was measured up at Halls, the drapers, on Monnow street which, even for those days, was a very old fashioned store specializing in haberdashery. When one purchased an item, the cash was put in a metal container and attached to a kind of conveyor belt near the ceiling where it ran along like a train to the cashier. Several minutes later, a ding would signal the return of the change—what were called coins of the "the Realm"— a combination of half-crowns, florins, shillings, sixpenny bits, threepenny bits, pennies, halfpennies, right down to the lowly farthing.

The first few days at my new school were very exciting as we learned the rules, and there were enough of my old friends from Overmonnow Girls' School to make me feel quite comfortable.

Friends at Monmouth School for Girls—I am seated second from the right.

The uniform—maroon gymslips in winter and red and white check dresses in summer—had to be worn to exacting standards—skirt hems at floor length when kneeling, straw boaters completely horizontal on our heads.

Everyone wore the same style of shoe—likely Buster Browns for which our feet were always X-rayed at Clark's shoe shop to make sure they were a good fit. What a thrill it was to see the bones in our feet, such a thrill that children often played on that machine while parents were being fitted for shoes themselves. Of course, it was inevitable that someone would spoil the fun and so it turned out when it was determined that the continual exposure to radiation was probably not such a bright idea.

We were instructed to have two pairs of shoes for gym—an indoor pair and an outdoor pair—called daps in Wales. Woe betide the person who was caught wearing outdoor daps indoors or indoor daps outdoors!

We walked to and from the bus through Monmouth in crocodile form—running was frowned upon—so very unladylike—and we were not allowed to talk in the street or enter a shop except with special permission which could be given only once a week. There were always prefects in charge, waiting to seize upon any miscreant who dared to defy the rules so that they could gleefully report back to our house mistresses the next day.

Imagine how foreign this all seemed to a ruffian who only months before had been involved in turf warfare in the streets of Monmouth against the girls from the council houses. Fitting into my new environment, I began to realize, would present some challenges.

Lunch was served in the school dining room and, again, silence was demanded until we were all seated, and then polite conversation was allowed only with the girl on either side or, if unfortunate in position in line, the teacher at the head of the table. No one was allowed to leave the table until every last morsel had been eaten.

Every Thursday, I had to exercise the skills of a magician to secrete chunks of overcooked, leathery liver into my gym-slip pocket and dispose of it in the toilet before it was discovered. The day that several large pieces were located under the table, smothered in a melting block of Wall's ice-cream, for which no one would admit ownership, the whole school body had to reassemble in our original spots until the culprit was ferreted out and suspended. That girl was lucky! The fifth-former who had been caught smoking in the toilet, the week before, had been shamed in front of the whole school assembly and expelled on the spot.

The headmistress, Agnes Flora MacDonald, a striking looking Scottish woman—tall and severe with a mass of snow-white hair piled high on her head—led the daily assembly. Peering disapprovingly at us over her glasses, she scanned the hall, as in eerie silence, hardly daring to breathe, we sat bolt upright in straight rows according to height.

Each day, a student had to take a turn accompanying her to lunch, to sit with her and the sixth form prefects on the head table. It was just one more failed scheme designed to turn me into a young lady. As our turn came around, we were instructed to initiate the conversation. What exactly did I have to talk about? There was little in my life that was fit for public consumption:

"Well, Miss MacDonald, my Grandma has been under the stairs, slitting her throat three times this week, what do you have to say to that?"

I still shudder at the thought of how I was stricken so rigid with fear that I could not utter an intelligible word and sat through the whole ordeal being ignored by Miss MacDonald accordingly, her stony silence conveying just how she felt about me.

The classes were streamed and the Eleven-Plus girls were automatically assigned to the B stream which was taught by the younger more inexperienced teachers. Once classed as the elite—superior to our old friends who had not passed the exam—we were then made to feel inferior to those in the A stream. At every stage, scorn and derision were heaped upon us from some quarter.

Haydn was the only one who bore me no ill will for being separated from him by an exam. He had inherited his mother's gentleness and kindness. He was quite content at the Secondary Modern School and proud of the fact that I had won a scholarship.

Hazel and I, however, grew further and further apart by a feeling of failure on her part rather than any feeling of superiority on mine. In her eyes, I had become a snob.

On our arrival, we had been put into one of four houses all of which had names of former baronets, or people of similar ilk, who had financially supported the school. Each group had a housemistress. Mine, Miss Whately, was even more intimidating than the headmistress.

Early on, I was isolated as a child who, if I was not to lower the tone of the school, needed to be brought up to a higher social status. Up against the moneyed, refined, sophisticated students with their element of snobbery, I was a rough-hewn, country bumpkin headed for social seclusion.

My first humiliation was being told that I would require elocution lessons. Miss MacDonald added, condescendingly, that since my mother was divorced and in no position to pay for the lessons, she would see to it that the school would cover the cost. How magnanimous of her!

ROSE DUDLEY

Miss MacDonald and Miss Whatley who preferred "polished" students

The lessons took place during the lunch hour which excluded me from team sports' practices and all activities with my friends. I was embarrassed to tell them to what I was being subjected, so understandably, they thought I was deliberately avoiding them. I began to be ostracized by the few friends I had made and accepted that even to them I had become an oddity.

The eventual outcome of the elocution lessons was that I no longer spoke in the coarse dialect of my family or former country friends, so my relatives made fun of me every time I opened my mouth, and Hazel and the rest of the "failures" saw it as a sure sign that I had become the snob that they had labelled me.

Feeling more and more of a misfit, I became increasingly withdrawn and painfully shy. I was ashamed of my family who, to my way of thinking, was the cause of my being thrust into this uncomfortable position. Instead of the staff having some empathy for my situation, many of them derided me for my shyness and lack of participation which was a sure way for me to disappear even deeper into my shell.

Why is it that so many teachers like to point out

weaknesses of which we are already so painfully aware? One comment that still sticks with me was,

"Rosie seems always to be on the fringe of things." I was, indeed, "on the fringe." I knew it, and it was not a comfortable feeling. I needed no reminder. Is a comment like that ever going to encourage one to dive immediately into the fray and become the centre of all activity? As a teacher, later in my life, it was a lesson to me to choose my words wisely.

Due to my athletic ability, largely thanks to a knife-wielding grandmother, I played on house teams in most of the sports—lacrosse, netball, rounders and cricket— and I soon began to gain some fame as a runner, but I shied away from attention and tended to avoid any situation in which I might excel. That led to my physical education teacher once writing on my report,

"Rosie lacks attack," another painful blow to me, but a comment which caused a great deal of mirth in the family.

Being dressed down by a teacher was such a common occurrence that cutting remarks have mostly been lost in the annals of history, but the following derisive words are recorded for their effrontery:

"You're a sloppy, spineless creature just mooning about in a passive sort of way who wouldn't put yourself out for anyone." That constitutes just a small sample of the admonishment delivered to me by my very professional and reputable housemistress for missing a games practice for a valid reason. She proved her point when, although I knew she was being unreasonable, I stood there in silence and did not try, in any way, to defend myself.

I wandered, or perhaps it would be more appropriate to say slithered back to my biology class, fighting back my tears, the embodiment of the invertebrates we were studying—spineless—one of the lower forms of life, drifting around in the darkest depths of my tortured existence.

I was filled with indignation for many years afterwards—my husband would say, "for life"—and fantasized about murdering my unfeeling house mistress, but age and wisdom have led me to believe that what she said, though cruel, was correct. That was exactly the way I was presenting myself to the world at that time, but my upbringing had rendered me powerless to do anything about it. I had had no voice for so many years that I ceased to imagine that I might have one.

I was ashamed of my home. I would not think of inviting anyone to visit, and I shied away from any relationship that might result in my being asked to another child's home and being unable to reciprocate. There were many children who were anxious to make friends with me on my arrival at the school, but if they lived out of my immediate neighbourhood, I made a point of avoiding them, leaving them wondering, no doubt, why I rejected their advances.

Having made every effort never to get myself into a compromising situation, my blood ran cold on one occasion, when I fell and injured my leg, and two of the teachers insisted on driving me home. I can never forget the discomfort I felt on that car journey and how, in my mind, I frantically tried to devise a plan to prevent them from taking me all the way home.

About a mile from the house, I persuaded them to stop the car, convincing them that it would be impossible to turn around further on. I assumed that they would drop me off and drive away, but they insisted on walking with me—as I tried to disguise the excruciating pain in my leg—all the way to the house where they could plainly see that several articulated vehicles would have had no difficulty turning around in the spacious motor-house yard.

I was dreading what I would find and that my grandmother would invite them in. I left them at the front door while I hobbled around to the back, sending chickens and ducks running and squawking in all directions and falling over those that were pecking away at the dinner plates, put down in the porch for the dogs and cats to lick. In a split second, I surveyed the whole scene in the kitchen. It was worse than I could ever have imagined.

My grandmother, as usual, clad in her apron, curlers and rubber boots, was feathering chickens into a metal bath in front of the fire. A flurry of feathers floated around the room, settling on her, the furniture, the picture frames and the line of wet washing sagging across the room. The smell of burning feathers was suffocating. Unburnt feathers were valiantly trying to escape from where they had become stuck in the soot at the back of the chimney. The naked bodies of two anaemic-looking, feathered chickens lay, legs splayed, on the oil-cloth covered table, their blood trickling in single drops over the edge into a pool on the floor. Two more blood-soaked chickens, awaiting their turn, lay on the floor beside the bathtub. My heart sank.

When I explained who was at the door, I saw my grandmother scramble towards the sewing machine, but then she appeared to have second thoughts. Even she must have realized that the addition of her false teeth was the last thing that was going to save this day.

After a very brief conversation and a cursory look at the scene that surrounded them, the teachers left, no doubt realizing why I had tried so hard to thwart them. It took my heart at least an hour to return to its normal place and speed. I was not able to look either teacher in the eye for many weeks following. I knew full well that my situation would have been the topic of conversation amongst the school staff for days. I had been exposed.

Realizing that my bizarre upbringing was largely responsible for my unhappiness at school, I felt my anger building at my grandmother's antics. Haydn continued to bait her, with predictable consequences, but I tried hard not to get embroiled in the battles. I became increasingly silent and morose and disappeared outside or upstairs to avoid the regular scenes. I began to build a protective wall around me.

Due to the lack of light, however, I was forced to do my homework at the kitchen table close to the Tilley lamp. How easy do you think it is to concentrate on math equations or the conjugation of French and Latin verbs while your grandmother is slitting her throat under the stairs? I begged Haydn to ignore her, but his quirky sense of humour, it seemed, would not allow him to miss any opportunity to annoy her. She became increasingly deranged.

Towards the end of the fifth form, students had to make some decisions about their future. I had always stated that I wished to become a teacher mainly because, in those days there did not seem to be too many options.

On informing Miss MacDonald of my goal, she was less than enthusiastic. She made it plain that I was an unsuitable candidate. My mother was summoned to the school for an interview which filled me with dread. I fretted about how she would dress and what sort of impression she would make. I prayed that she wouldn't arrive in Wellington boots covered in cow dung and her soiled old mac and headscarf. I had no empathy for what such an interview would have meant for her. It was probably the hardest thing she had been forced to do since informing Mr. Williams of my departure from Tregare school. She, like me, was intimidated by anyone in authority.

Miss MacDonald explained that my desire to become a teacher would require a good deal of work on all our parts. I was "a rough diamond" she explained, who needed more than a bit of polishing. The elocution lessons would now be given more frequently:

"I know that you are in no position to afford them, Mrs. Lynch, but the school is prepared to cover the cost so you do not have to worry about the expense." she said, in a voice laden with insincerity. I was mortified and assumed that my mother would take offence at the condescending tone, but, again, she thought it all quite hilarious, as if she was entirely removed from any responsibility in the scene that was being played out.

Miss MacDonald went on to explain that it would be unlikely that I would be accepted at any teachers' college in my present uncivilized state, so it would be unwise to apply. With those hurtful words, any last remnants of self-esteem vanished.

My mother and I went home in silence, but as I did my piano practice that evening, and my mother laughingly gave a report of Miss MacDonald's words to the family, my secret tears fell silently and steadily onto the keys.

I was a conscientious student, finding that immersing myself in my studies was a good antidote to my social and emotional issues, and so I passed with ease, all seven of my O-Levels, the only qualifications that I needed for entry into a teachers' college. At that point, I could have left the school and gained some life experience away from my bizarre home and family.

I applied and was accepted to be a teachers' aide at a private school in southern England. I was uplifted by the thought of escaping from what had become such a miserable existence, but it was my grandmother who took control and decided that it was a mistake for me to leave school until I had taken A-Levels. My mother, weak and powerless to intervene, let her have the last word.

Partly out of resentment, and partly because I was then seventeen and beginning to enjoy a social life outside of school, I became less conscientious over my studies. I also made a regrettable error in judgment over the courses I chose to study in the sixth form.

ROSE DUDLEY

I was passionate about English Literature and French, but the girls who had signed up for those subjects were potential Oxford and Cambridge entrants who all had the right accent and who intimidated me. Thus, I ended up choosing subjects which didn't particularly interest me, based solely on whom I would feel more comfortable with in my classes.

The school motto was "Serve and Obey" and was emblazoned across the school as well as on the pocket of our blazers, in the unlikely event that we forgot. Our patron saint was Catherine of Alexandria. She was a Christian saint and a virgin who was martyred in the fourth century. She was also known as St. Catherine of the Wheel and Catherine the Great Martyr. She was scourged, imprisoned, tortured and condemned to death on the spiked breaking wheel. My life at Monmouth School for Girls, I thought, bore an uncanny resemblance to hers. The choice of her as our saint was in no way surprising.

There was a hymn that we sang to her also, but I have mostly forgotten the words and can find no reference to them. I wouldn't be surprised if it was composed by one of our more masochistic teachers—the lyrics, I recall, spoke of anguish, hunger, suffering and death.

In preparation for St. Catherine's Day, which fell on the twenty-fifth of November, we were given ballroom dancing lessons. Monmouth Boys' School was only a stone's throw away at the bottom of the hill, so it would have seemed sensible to invite the boys up to be our practise partners, but we were kept isolated from them always. You never know what mingling with boys might have led to. We had to be content to dance with each other, half of us taking the male role. I suppose, however, that I must thank St. Catherine, for I did become reasonably proficient at the Waltz, the Quickstep and the Gay Gordons, and this, it is true, stood me in excellent stead for the Saturday night Young Farmers' hops.

So many people talk of school days being the happiest of their lives, but the day I left Monmouth School for Girls was not a sad day for me. I have never ever set foot in those halls since, and I'm only in touch with two former pupils, more through coincidence than by design.

One of those, Di Clark, lived on a big farm in the area. My aunt Phyllis was hired as a nanny for her and her sister when they were growing up which I thought automatically made us subservient to their family.

The girls, Diane and Judith, were always dressed so beautifully and their mother appeared so sophisticated in her riding gear that to my child's eyes they were members of the upper-class. It was, therefore, a shock for me to learn that my perception of her family was completely wrong. They were tenant farmers whose lives, apart from the mental asylum component, mirrored ours. Di's experiences of and thoughts about the school are the same as mine.

It is unfortunate that so many negative experiences tend to overshadow anything positive. There were several younger teachers at the school who could be considered human: one who made French lessons so enjoyable and on whom I had a schoolgirl crush, an English teacher who brought Shakespearean tragedy alive and inspired my reading and a desire to write, another gifted lady who made history so fascinating and the sewing and cookery teacher who so kindly provided me with a safe haven in my times of distress.

Di and I have shared our stories on many occasions, now able to come to terms with the way we were treated. On leaving school, one assumes that one will be shown out the door with some words of wisdom to carry one through life. I remember no words of wisdom from any of the staff, but Di remembers Miss Whatley—

our infamous house mistress—telling her, as she departed those hallowed halls, that it would be her duty to stand at her parents' grave and throw earth on the coffin. It would be irreverent of me to tell you what I would like to have thrown on Miss Whatley's coffin.

"No one saves us but ourselves. No one can and no one may. We ourselves must walk the path."

I found those words of Buddha recently and thought how relevant they are but, at the same time, how long and arduous that path can be when one must navigate one's way through the British class system.

It is unfortunate that as children we are without the wisdom that can only come through experience whether it be bitter or otherwise. Only on reflection, do we realize that it is our own behaviour—lack of confidence and self-esteem—that leads others to treat us as they do. We must, despite our life's experience, take responsibility for our own destiny, as challenging as that may be.

It is only on reflection, also, that despite my unhappy years at Monmouth School for Girls, I know that I am where I am today because of the opportunity to attend such a prestigious institution. The humiliation was not to my liking, but the school, despite what my husband says, did succeed in taking quite a bit of the country out of the girl.

MEMOIR OF "A SLOPPY, SPINELESS, CREATURE"

CHAPTER TWELVE

"No matter where you are or where you grow up, you always go through the same awkward moments of being a teenager and growing up and trying to figure out who you are."
Aimee Teegarden

In and out of school, I spent my teenage years feeling embarrassed about my family, my home, my looks, my clothes, my whole being—everything. I had to wait until I had teenagers myself to realize that even in the best of circumstances, this is just the natural order of things.

When I was growing up, discussing one's feelings was out of the question. I kept all my emotions securely locked inside an impenetrable vault. It was what I had learned from my family. I could have felt so much better sharing my inner thoughts and realizing that so many others felt just as ugly, miserable and lonely, hated themselves as thoroughly and had the same urge to murder members of the family and the school staff.

I did not enjoy a close relationship with my mother. I felt that she was entirely responsible for my situation, and there was undoubtedly a great deal of unspoken resentment on my part. Her inability to discuss her feelings and the taciturnity with which she lived her life was beyond her control. She had been badly scarred by her mother's treatment of her and seemed unable to recover. But why did I have to experience being a mother before I showed any understanding of what it was like to live in her shoes? I know she tried her best to be a good mother, and this became evident when I saw her kind and loving interactions with her grandchildren. I know now that our lack of closeness was more to do with my fragile self-image rather than any lack of love on her part.

Discussion of bodily functions was taboo in those days, and was a source of acute embarrassment to my family, so when I began to menstruate, I could never have discussed it with my mother or she with me. I dealt with it myself in the way that many country people were still dealing with it in the early fifties—with rags from the rag bag—hence the origin of the whispered saying, "she's on the rags"—or sheep wool of which there was always a plentiful supply on the barbed wire fences and hedges around the farm—primitive, you may well think, but much better than the alternative—folded pages from *The Farmer's Weekly*.

My mother eventually must have sensed what was happening, for some months later, an unmarked, brown-paper-wrapped package of sanitary pads appeared in my underwear drawer, but not a word was exchanged between us—the embarrassment of silence, a greater oppression.

To be fair to my mother, however, and to put things in perspective, there was still an unbelievable level of awkwardness surrounding this normal monthly occurrence. Many people were too embarrassed to have to ask for sanitary pads in the chemists' shops—it wasn't possible to pick up packages from the shelves as it is today.

The Kotex advertisement in 1946 declared, "Your secret is safe with us because Kotex has flat pressed ends that don't show," a Modess advertisement in 1949 boasted, "It is wrapped to look like a box of note paper or bath salts or candy or facial tissue—actually, it's Modess in the wonderful new-shaped box," and Modess, again, was advertised as "the pad for the upper-class," through the 40s, 50s, and right into the 60s.

I was, I suppose, what is referred to as "a late developer," so I didn't enter the social scene, such as it was in Tregare, until I was around seventeen or eighteen. The social scene at my school had all taken place on that one day of the year—St. Catherine's Day—the twenty-fifth of November—but, at least, it had been the means by which I had learned to dance.

I loved to dance, and there were plenty of opportunities in the villages beyond Tregare. Some of the boys were, by then, able to drive, and one or two of them even owned a car; Tregare was beginning to enter the modern age.

Every weekend, there would be a Young Farmers' dance and always someone willing to transport me. Tony Bradley was still in love with me so he was always more than eager. I still only thought of him as a good friend, but as he was an exceptional dancer, he was always my favourite partner. Together, completely in sync, we literally flew around the dance floor.

Bill Haley and the Comets and Tommy Steele had arrived on the scene in the late fifties:

"What 'ad the bloody world come to?" but since, in my house, we were only allowed to have the radio tuned to the B.B.C. Home Service and turned on only for the daily news, I was well protected from their evil influence.

My grandmother always demanded silence when the daily news was on, but her understanding of world affairs was limited by her bigoted view that Britain was always in the right. While British children grew up indoctrinated to believe that our country made wise decisions that benefitted the whole world, even I had a slight problem during the Suez Crisis in 1956 accepting that,

"Some bugger should shoot off that bloody ol' Nasser's B.A.L.L.S."

Now that my horizons were widening, I began to get to know boys from other villages. One, Edwin, who had lived his whole life only about three miles across the fields, but whom I had never known, became my regular date.

The Bradleys had literally soared into the modern age with the installation of a telephone, so our dates were arranged through Tony who would receive the call from Edwin and come running across the fields to let me know the plans for the following Saturday. How hard that must have been for him and how unintentionally cruel it was of me.

I had no romantic interest in Edwin or any other boy. In fact, both Haydn and I were terrified of the opposite sex. Though all my girlfriends who met Haydn developed crushes on him, he never, to my knowledge, had a real girlfriend in his whole life. But, what do I know? It just may be one more of those well-kept family secrets. Although we were the closest of friends we, like the rest of the family, stayed well away from any personal conversations.

Listening to my grandmother spelling out the word S E X in hushed whispers, and with such distaste, and observing the animals following their instincts in the fields—our only sex education—made the whole business seem quite repulsive. Besides, all the country boys smelled of a putrid mixture of tractor oil, stale milk, cowsheds and Brylcream, so dancing with them was as close as one would ever want to get.

My grandmother had so closely monitored all her daughters' comings and goings, though to no good effect, but there were no restrictions whatsoever on Haydn and me. We came in at all hours of the morning, but I could have assured her that she didn't have a thing to worry about.

I must have been a huge disappointment to Edwin who never could advance beyond snogging and a valiant attempt at groping. I had to let him kiss me, as disgusting as it was, as I needed to ensure my continued transportation to the dances, but I made him keep his hands firmly to himself.

Writing about what I believed was my unusual level of naivety reminded me of a story related to me by my late friend, Maggie Cary, a nurse, who had been working in a men's ward for several years and was obviously extremely familiar with male anatomy. Her date, getting a little amorous one evening, exposed his penis. She said, still conveying her horror,

"It was the first social penis I had ever seen in my life, and I was so utterly shocked that I told him to put it away immediately."

Apparently, he complied. I shuddered for her, relieved that I had not had to witness such an abomination at that guileless stage in my life.

I did, however, have my schoolgirl crushes on film stars. I often went to the cinema with girlfriends, mostly a school friend, Susan, who was also in love with Haydn and spent many weekends cycling from her house to mine—some ten miles or more—in hopes of winning him over, but to no avail.

Sometimes, I went with another friend, a vicar's daughter. Like other vicars' offspring I have known, she was living life on the wild side. It was fortunate that my grandmother didn't know what she was up to. As an influence, she was far more dangerous than Bill Haley or Tommy Steele.

It still only cost about nine pence or a shilling, about 25 cents, to go to the cinema, the only entertainment that we could afford. We were hopelessly in love with Kenneth More and Dirk Bogarde and didn't miss any of the films in which they starred. Together, we cried our way through Reach for the Sky, A Night to Remember—the original story of the Titanic, Ill met by Moonlight, A Tale of Two Cities and The Wind Cannot Read.

Meanwhile, the boys were fawning over the bodies of Brigitte Bardot, Sophia Loren and Gina Lollobrigida.

Just as we had, as children, gone on Sunday School outings to the sea, as teenagers, we went on similar Young Farmers' trips. There was not a repeat of the kind of travel sickness involving buckets, but I do remember that on more than one occasion the driver had to stop the bus for someone to get off to be sick because of drinking too much beer. I also recall the girls who were snogging in the back seat, but I had no time for such shenanigans.

Returning from one of those trips, I arrived home to learn that my grandfather had died. Other than the King's demise, it was the first time I had been exposed to the death of anyone. He had been ill with prostate cancer but was recovering and was not expected to die. He had passed away suddenly that day of a pulmonary embolism. I was absolutely shattered. I felt such a wave of sadness for him—that he had experienced so little love in his life.

As Haydn and I walked in, the whole family was slumped around the kitchen table with pale, tear-stained faces. Aunt Blodwen, who had been called from her place of work to assume her usual role, was tapping her fingers on the arms of her chair, as if making decisions on what had to be done about the situation that had so suddenly occurred.

Chunks of dried out cheese, meat and bread, and cups of cold tea sat untouched on the oil-cloth covered table. The fire had died in the grate creating a deathly chill in the room. My grandmother was quietly weeping. It was the first time I had ever seen her express any strong emotion other than anger. Perhaps, in her own strange way, she had loved my grandfather after all.

There was a curious irony in his death. Only months before my grandfather's funeral, a new burial ground had been consecrated at the church, and as we stood there for the ceremony, my grandfather had asked the other church warden, Mr. Jenkins, his employer, who he thought would be the first one in the new churchyard. As it turned out, it was Mr. Jenkins followed almost immediately by my grandfather. They had been such firm friends and had worked side by side for much of their lives and now it seems so fitting that they lie side by side for eternity.

My grandfather's funeral was the first one that I had ever attended. It was such a morbid affair—the likes of which could only be staged by the Welsh—and officiated by the Reverend Phillips who could be depended upon to deliver the message in the worst possible light.

Soon after the funeral, a representative from the church came to the house with an envelope containing parochial charity which was given annually to the poor of the village. It had been decided that my grandmother was now a deserving case. That was the one and only occasion when I saw her show her real self to the outside world. She was furious that anyone would think of her as a charity case or that she would accept something for nothing. She told that astonished gentleman, in no uncertain terms, in what part of his anatomy he could stick his envelope. No one was ever going to believe that *she* couldn't fend for herself. She was mortally offended, and we didn't ever hear the end of it. She wasn't trying to teach us a lesson, but, indirectly, it was a good one to learn. I did admire her for her pride and her fierce independence.

I still attended church on Sundays. Despite my trial-by-fire introduction to religion, I adored the hymns, the more mournful the better.

After Aunt Maisie had flown the coop to become a bus conductress, I inherited the job of organist. I had no innate talent whatsoever, but I had been forced to take years of lessons from Gwladys Shipway who seemed to believe that a good rap across the knuckles for every wrong note would produce musical prodigies. What a terrible disappointment her life must have been! Still, I could manage to hammer out the hymns, pedalling furiously on the old harmonium while Mrs. Phillips, the Reverend Phillips's wife, sang lustily enough to drown out any wrong notes and give the impression that the church was full to capacity.

The Rev. Phillips's demeanour had not softened

since my Sunday School days. He still shouted from the pulpit at the largely empty pews insinuating that those present were entirely responsible for the absence of the crowd as well as the crucifixion of Jesus. No matter how insulting he was, the few devout parishioners, just like us, when we attended Sunday School, kept coming back for more verbal abuse.

One of the ladies in a neighbouring village produced a church pantomime each year and during my last year of high school, she invited me to play a role. I remember it only because of an incident that reduced me to a feeling of utter worthlessness.

As we practised, it became increasingly obvious that the producer's lack of talent was only outmatched by the lack of that of the performers. What was unclear, bearing that in mind, was why I was given a singing role.

On the night of the performance, Aunt Marion, whose singing I had so much admired as a child, was in the front row of the audience. As I opened my mouth for the first musical number, she exclaimed, in a booming voice that echoed around the entire hall,

"Oh, My God, she's going to sing!"

Aunt Marion, as much as her self-esteem had been battered by her own mother, has inherited some of her worst traits. I have tackled her about her lack of tact on many occasions, but she hotly denies that she ever said what she did.

Haydn and I continued to help on the farm and, armed with my lessons from my days at Tregare School, I was a skilled worker. I have always craved neatness and order and, although that could be a challenge at Oakdale, I managed to markedly improve the property. My husband, who has found my attention to detail extremely annoying, believes that I have a disorder which he calls "critical eye syndrome." It can be a bane in one's life, but at Oakdale it was an asset.

We were still called on to take and fetch the

animals to pasture and to keep up the vow of silence with Nellie Powell. We helped to treat the sheep for foot-rot which was so common that, even though I only remember sunny days, that was evidence enough that it rained a lot in Wales. We were also there to hold the sheep down while my mother immunized them against liver fluke, and perhaps tetanus, to which they are prone.

In need of some pocket money, I took on jobs outside the home—picking peas for the Bradleys, followed by digging potatoes. I also spent a summer working on the hardware counter in Woolworths.

My old housemistress came in, and although she must have recognized me, she chose to pretend otherwise. I believe she assumed that I had become a permanent employee so took a dim view of me ending up in what she would have considered to be a menial job after being educated for seven years in such a prestigious establishment. I let her believe it. Her presence still filled me with anger.

Why didn't I have the courage to tell her how her cruel words had affected me? Why didn't I have the audacity to tell her that she should be ashamed to call herself a teacher or that she was a bitter and twisted old spinster? Perhaps, because I was still possessed of the label that she had bestowed upon me. Perhaps, because I already realized that she had been right.

During several vacations, I worked as a waitress in hotels far away from home where I made friends with girls from other parts of the country. They all had the delightful, regional accents of their area. No one could determine, from my phony accent, where I came from.

In my last year of high school, I applied to teachers' colleges and, subsequently, was summoned for an interview in Bristol. To avoid the risk of further humiliation, I decided not to tell the headmistress.

I was eighteen years old and quite capable of going alone to the interview, but, despite my protestations,

Aunt Blodwen was called upon to be my chaperone. I already had Miss MacDonald's words to fret about, but to arrive at an interview with an aunt, especially that one, in tow, I thought would be the kiss of death.

As if that wasn't enough, my grandmother insisted that I should wear a hat so, duly, my mother took me to Monmouth to buy one. As Halls, the drapers, was our only choice of shop, there was nothing remotely suitable. That did not deter my mother who settled on a red velvet number that looked like a museum piece. It was a museum piece. It was badly faded on one side from being displayed in a south facing window for many years. It sat on the top of my head resembling a large lump of cow's liver. I was mortified. With that and a new coat that would have been more suitable for a 70-year-old, I looked like a complete freak—one of those unfortunates who, in less politically correct times, they used to put in a booth and charge money for people to see at a funfair:

"Come and see the bearded lady, hurry in to see the two-headed dwarf."

Why not come in to see the freak with her liver growing on top of her head while you are at it, I was thinking to myself.

On the bus to Newport, I reflected on the scene which had unfolded when I had been in a comparable situation—the occasion of Aunt Phyllis's wedding. Without any consultation, my mother had bought me a mustard yellow coat and matching hat. It was the most unsightly outfit that had ever seen the light of day. I was being forced to wear it over a dress that was five inches longer than the coat. It made me look educationally sub-normal, if I can be forgiven, for a moment, for lapsing into political incorrectness.

I decided it was time to put my foot down; I flatly refused to put it on. My grandmother was incensed. She took the stick down from the mantelpiece and brandished it in front of my face:

"You brazen little 'ussy, you ungrateful little bitch, I knew it was a mistake to take you in, you with your 'igh and mighty ideas. Go back to your drunken father, in the gutter where you belong, I 'ave a good mind to give that coat away to 'azel Bradley." she screamed. I could not contain myself:

"Go right ahead, you know Hazel wouldn't be seen dead in it," I screamed back, surprising even myself. The inevitable scene followed so, defeated once more, I gave in.

Here is "the brazen little hussy" in the infamous outfit.

When I arrived at the college, I managed, with a great deal of negotiation, to deposit my aunt on a bench behind a thick bush, well out of sight of the entrance. She was extremely annoyed. She carried her customary air of importance about her and seriously thought that she would improve my chances of acceptance if she could be seen. I knew otherwise.

To my surprise, the interview went very well, despite the outfit, and I was encouraged by the kindness and the humour of the staff who interviewed me. They smiled and even laughed on occasion. They were normal, decent human beings. This was something that I was not expecting at all—certainly not what I had been accustomed to.

When the letter came to say that I had been accepted, I was beside myself with joy. I could not wait to inform the headmistress.

Miss MacDonald gushed and said that she was so pleased for me, but I felt that she was almost disappointed that she had been proven wrong, and I am sure she was concerned about what the college might have been thinking about the calibre of students that her school was turning out.

It was just months before I could put the degradation suffered at Haberdashers' Monmouth School for Girls behind me. In July, I walked down the driveway for the last time. I didn't glance back. I looked forward to a new chapter beginning in October of 1960.

CHAPTER THIRTEEN

"You have brains in your head
You have feet in your shoes
You can steer yourself
In any direction you choose.
You're on your own,
And you know what to do,
You are the guy
Who'll decide where to go."
Dr. Seuss

At my interview, I had been asked if I would prefer to study at Barrow Court, the rural branch of the college in Somerset, which concentrated more on outdoor studies. That seemed like the best option for a country girl.

During the summer months, I vacillated between excitement and apprehension. This was to be a fresh start where no one knew about me or my past. I wanted to get off on the right foot. I now had an acceptable, if phony, accent which was a step in the right direction.

Barrow Court

I had no idea what to expect, so when I arrived in late September, I was completely in awe of the beauty and absolute perfection of the college building and its surroundings. It was a scene straight from the pages of a Jane Austen novel.

Barrow Court has a long and fascinating history. It was first mentioned in the Domesday Book. It was originally a Benedictine nunnery, by the order of St John, in 1196, apparently, a refuge for a small number of unwanted daughters. Prior knowledge of that fact could have been a little disconcerting. Before it became a teacher training college, just after WWII it had been a convalescent home for wounded soldiers.

Most of the later buildings dated back to Victorian times, but there were still remnants of the Elizabethan period—the plaster ceilings and some of the wood panelling in the larger staterooms.

The gardens, which rivalled some of the famous, ornate gardens of Europe, had been laid out by Inigo Thomas, from 1890 to 1900, with romantic pavilions, steps, ponds and terraces. There were so many nooks and crannies in which to lose oneself entirely, and some very interesting statuary, the most impressive being the twelve women representing the stages of life from youth to old age. It summoned romance.

Our favourite haunt would become the Shrubbery— our very own secret garden. It never would have occurred to me, at the time, that all kinds of sexual exploits could have been going on there. I automatically assumed that everyone else was as innocent as I.

The college was accessed by a narrow, flower bedecked lane from the "Clist and Rattle" garage on the main Bristol to Weston-Super-Mare road. We walked that lane so many times in different seasons, breathing in the scent of wild flowers in spring and marvelling at the hedges of ripened rose hips entwined in old man's beard in the autumn. I remember the winter of 1962 when, returning after the Christmas break, we trudged through drifts of pure, untouched snow six feet deep, stretching between the hedgerows.

At the end of the lane was the lodge signalling the entrance to the college, a sturdy stone structure—a stately home in its own right. From there, a long driveway led up to a circular courtyard at the front door. A Cedar of Lebanon tree, dating back 500 years, framed the driveway on approach.

I arrived, on that first day, with a trunk filled mostly with textbooks along with a vast number of novels that we were to have read prior to arrival, but that load was trifling compared to the heavy burden weighing upon my heart.

Three staff members immediately took us under their wings like mother hens.

Dagmar Andersen, originally from Australia, our "loco parentis" figure, was the warden. She was a small, attractive, dark haired, soft spoken woman with a permanent half smile. She seemed very remote, but she had such an understanding of young people. Her approach was always heralded by a low cough, as if she tactfully wished not to discover a student doing anything that might embarrass herself. She was insistent on standards though, and got very upset, for instance, if she encountered someone with a cup but no saucer. Her favourite rejoinder was,

"Standards, ladies, don't forget."

She had the most extensive library. Her sombre study was wall to wall books, a collection that would make any small-town library pale in comparison. I have no doubt that she had read every single one. She loved poetry and had memorized the complete works of many of the famous English poets.

We always have regrets in life, and one of mine is that I was too shy to get to know Miss Andersen better— my emotionally bereft existence continued to rob me of the ability to develop an intimate relationship with anyone. When she died, one of the students, Sally Stirrit, who had kept in close contact with her through the years following student days, wrote the following tribute to her:

"Au Revoir Dear Friend
I feel your constant presence,
Watching over me and guiding,
Steadfast in your care,
For you never liked saying "Goodbye"
Forgive me for not being there, yet wanting you still to be;
You understand how much I cared,
How I miss you now you are gone.
You found peace here and eternally
The haven of your garden, lovingly tended and enjoyed.
Your favourite poets, Auden, Yeats and Gunn,
Plays, television and your cats,
You lived your life for others
Through your simple faith in God.
I cannot call you back.
Mine only to relive all our memories
Accepting your death through poetry,
My humble tribute to you."

I wish, so much, that I could have been able to write a beautiful tribute like that myself.

Most people were in awe of Miss Ruth Jelley, the straight-laced biology teacher and gardening instructor. She could be rather intimidating as she approached in her tweeds and Wellington boots, a heavy scowl on her ruddy face, but I won favour with her very early on when, on a farm walk, I casually strolled up to stroke a cow while other girls from the city were giddily screeching in fear.

"Miss Lynch," she cried excitedly, "I believe you must have been brought up amongst animals."

Little did she realize how close that was to the truth.

Miss Jelley originally owned an old, black Lab called Treasure. We all went into mourning on the occasion of Treasure's death, but shortly afterwards, he was replaced with a wild, little Basset Hound named Lollipop, best known for tearing through the halls rucking up the carpets. One could score lots of points by making a huge fuss of Miss Jelley's dogs.

She also kept a very vicious Belgian hare in a cage behind the stables and, at times, girls were asked to clean out its cage which was not at all to the liking of the hare. Several girls had been mauled, and Miss Jelley herself had been taken to hospital to have stitches in her leg following an attack by that ungrateful creature.

A highly intelligent woman, Miss Jelley took a very dim view of our lack of general knowledge. Her most common question to us was,

"How can you ladies have lived so long and learned so little?"

Sadly, she had a stroke only about seven years after I left Barrow. She chose to be buried in Barrow churchyard. Years later, a former student, Reg Harris, would write,

"Miss Jelley is forever at Barrow Court, even though the rest of us can only live there in our memories."

In recent years, I stood by her grave remembering how I had admired and respected her.

Mrs. Gibbs, the matron, was the epitome of motherliness and kindness. A petite, smiling, attractive lady with perfect deportment, she marched briskly through the halls, a model of efficiency.

These three, dear women together provided a vital framework of security for us, and again, I regret that I never had the courage to tell any of them, at the time, what a positive effect they were having on my life.

At a fiftieth college reunion, I, and a group of friends, visited Mrs. Gibbs who, by that time, was 92 and in a retirement home in Clevedon. Unfortunately, she had nurtured so many students at the college, for so many years, that it was hard for her to place us. On my return to Canada, I sent her photographs along with a letter telling her how much I appreciated my years in her care, but it would have meant nothing to her at that stage. I was sad but not surprised to receive no reply.

Canon Sturdy was the college chaplain and the rector of the parish church. His jet-black hair was parted severely down the middle. He always looked mildly bemused and seemed, mostly, to be in a world of his own—perhaps communing with God. He had a habit of falling asleep anywhere at any time.

He was responsible for our spiritual health, although most of us were much too flighty and superficial to appreciate his valiant efforts on our behalf. Apart from a few who had accepted Jesus as their personal saviour, the majority of us were far beyond saving.

On my return for a thirtieth reunion, he conducted the service in the chapel. Seeing him hobbling in with the help of a cane, then in his seventies, his jet-black hair having turned snowy white, I was reduced to floods of tears, overcome by the stark realization of the passing of time and the inevitability of aging and death.

The only fly in the ointment at Barrow was Iris Congleton, the Childhood Education lecturer and, to my consternation, my personal tutor. She was a rough, mannish individual, with dark blond hair pulled back severely in a bun, who clomped around in size twelve brogues. She had a voice like a foghorn and referred to us only by our surnames. I thought she would have fitted in well at Monmouth School for Girls, not there in that gentle, nurturing establishment.

I shuddered whenever I heard her voice bellowing, "Lynch!" through the halls. She could make me feel immediately on the defensive and stop me in my tracks. She put the fear of God into almost everyone except one of the more mature students, Jan Oxley, who flatly refused to be intimidated by her. Jan would challenge her at every step and, thus, earned her respect, and Jan's mine.

The wonderful staff at Barrow—left to right—Mrs. Gibbs, Miss Jelley, Miss Andersen, Canon Sturdy and my nemesis—Miss Congleton. Lollipop lies at Mrs. Gibbs' feet

Every week, we met for afternoon tea and conversation. Entering the lounge for the first session, Miss Whatley's words were echoing in my head. I wanted, so desperately, to present myself as a different person—to change my ways—to expunge the memories, but I was so intimidated by this person who symbolized my history that I sat there mute, held captive by the past. Miss Congleton was not one to gently coax me into the conversation, so I agonized over those weekly meetings, plagued by my silence.

Two visiting lecturers came each week. Miss Bevir, a short haired, energetic sprite in a black leotard taught physical education and reminded us to be B.K.J—brisk, keen and jolly as she always was herself, and Miss

Williams, who taught dance in the Elizabethan tithe barn for which we were required to wear unflattering dance tunics with passion killing, matching bloomers in turquoise, red or yellow—outfits that made us feel anything but brisk, keen and jolly.

On our arrival, we were assigned rooms. Those, like me, who had no siblings, were automatically put in single rooms which was well intentioned, but not what I would have chosen. The girls who were two, three or four to a room quickly became close friends. Once more, I was "on the fringe."

Most of the other students were from lower-middle-class families, so with my cultured accent, I was accepted, on the surface, and no longer felt quite like the misfit I had been at school.

One of the girls who befriended me early on was clearly from an upper-middle-class family, judging by her accent. Some weeks after our arrival at the college, she accompanied me to meet my mother who had come to visit for the first time. Instantly, my friend recognized, by the way she was dressed and the way that she spoke, that my mother was a country peasant, and I witnessed my friend's attitude immediately changing towards me.

My mother had kindly brought me some items of makeup—lipstick, eyeshadow, foundation cream—very acceptable to an impecunious student. Following my mother's departure, my friend came to see what she had brought. Picking up the makeup and looking at the brand, she scoffed disgustedly,

"What cheap muck!" and tossed it down on my desk. Her words sliced through me like a knife—thoughtless words quickly said and immediately forgotten by a priggish individual—injurious words never forgotten by a fragile soul. I watched our developing friendship gradually diminishing as my baggage weighed more heavily upon me.

I welcomed the friendship of another Rosie, until I began to feel strangely uncomfortable in her presence. Being still a very naive country girl, I had never heard of lesbians. It wasn't until I turned 20 and saw the movie, "The World of Susie Wong," that I finally understood that "batting for the other side" didn't mean abandoning the English cricket team to play for Australia or South Africa.

I have often thought how difficult life must have been for Rosie at a time when sexual differences were not accepted as they are today. Like me, she had experienced social exclusion, but for different reasons. How many other girls had she approached and suffered rejection? How long had she been guarding her secret? I wondered if she had summoned up the courage to tell her parents. She found a partner in our second year, when the new intake of girls arrived, but it was not a relationship that she could celebrate openly. She had to sneak about to the whispering and tittering and the cruel statements of other students. Thankfully, we now live in more enlightened times.

Friends at Barrow—left to right—Pauline, Jan, Ros, me, Margaret

Our few simple chores consisted of telephone duty, setting tables and washing up at weekends, otherwise, we were waited on hand and foot. It was better than living at home for the majority. It was the Garden of Eden for me.

The rules were somewhat antiquated, but, as long as we adhered strictly to them, which I always did, everything went smoothly. We were not allowed to leave our rooms after 10:00 p.m. We could wear trousers in the confines of our room only. Curfew was at a ridiculously early hour—around 9:30 p.m.—although, once a week, we could get a special pass until 11:00 p.m. and once or twice a term, a pass for a much later hour so that we could attend special events. When that occurred, a staff member would have to wait up for us.usually Miss Andersen or the Major who lived at the lodge. Even though it was often very late, neither of them would fail to ask us about our evening and would manage to pretend that they were not just dying to get to bed.

The early curfew presented quite a problem as the college was a bus journey from Bristol, followed by the long walk from the main road which prevented us doing anything that happened after 8:30 p.m. That covered almost every possibility.

Soon after my arrival, I had a date with a student who took me to see Psycho. He, understandably, was furious when we had to leave the theatre just before the climax.

Because of the stringent hours, we were always referred to as "The Girls from the Nunnery." There was also a mental institution in the village of Barrow Gurney and I think some of the university students believed we were inmates from there.

During my second year, some leniency was shown over the trousers issue. We were permitted to wear them for Saturday morning gardening sessions as long as we took them off immediately afterwards, unless, of course, we did not leave our rooms. It defied logic that we could be seen anywhere around the college in those passion-killing dance outfits but not in trousers.

We ate in the oak-panelled dining room, always at the same table which was where many life-long friendships developed. The meals were excellent—breakfasts of eggs, bacon, baked beans and delicious fried bread, a full lunch with lots of casseroles and crumbles smothered in custard, and high tea where copious quantities of bread and dripping, fish paste, jam and marmite were consumed. Despite all that wonderful comfort food, my friend Margaret's husband, Tom, only remembers being served ice cream on hot plates.

As had been the custom at Monmouth School for Girls, we took turns sitting at the head table with the staff, having been invited to drink sherry with them beforehand. We were beginning to be treated like adults.

The commonly held belief that girls go to college only to find a husband appeared to be the case at Barrow. Within the first month, young men were literally beating down the doors, and students were pairing off. One could almost hear the sound of wedding bells in the far distance.

Tom was one of the first on the scene. No doubt, he had sampled many hot plates of ice cream and who knows what other delicacies by the first Christmas. He was a brusque, no-nonsense northerner who I thought would have been a good candidate for a soap-box on Hyde Park corner. He had been tipped off by a friend of his that Barrow was the best source of available "birds." I dated Tom briefly, though I have no memory of it and neither has he, so our brief dalliance was clearly not earth shattering for either of us. He then went on to break the record for the greatest number of Barrow "birds" dated in the shortest period, until he met the girl of his dreams, Margaret Perren, to whom he has been happily married for over 50 years. Margaret was a petite, pretty girl with dark hair, rosy cheeks and a permanent smile. She bounced rather than walked which matched her temperament entirely.

Tom was a student of veterinary medicine and his friend, John, was already dating a Barrow "bird," although I was unaware of it until one dull, rainy Saturday afternoon he arrived in the dining hall with her. Students could bring guests for meals a limited number of times on weekends.

He sat down right opposite me. He was so charismatic, had an enchanting smile, which revealed beautiful, even, white teeth, twinkling blue eyes and a heavy lick of light brown hair which fell to one side of his forehead. Oozing charm from every pore, he engaged in easy conversation with the girls at the table and soon became the centre of attention with his humour and infectious laughter. He won the hearts of all of us. How could one not be drawn to such a character? I was completely smitten, giddy, entranced. It was the first time in my life that I had been attracted to anyone of the opposite sex. I was in love, and I could tell that, although I had the sophistication of a cabbage and the dress sense of a cave woman, he felt the same way about me.

He had the mien of the wealthy country squire— dressed in a Harris tweed sports jacket, perfectly laundered shirt, old boys' tie and grey flannels. He looked nothing like a typical student, so I was surprised to learn that he was Tom's friend, discoverer of Barrow's never ending source of "birds," and, like Tom, studying veterinary medicine.

Apart from a strong Leicestershire accent, which I found appealing, he carried off the part of the well-bred English country gentleman to a tee.

At the end of the meal, the warden asked all visitors to leave the room so that she could address the students. A few other males quickly stood, scraping their chairs noisily on the oak floor and scurried out with heads low, but the object of my desire moved affectedly towards the door, bowed gracefully to the warden and, with a captivating smile, backed out, charming her and every girl in the room.

Following the meal, we all returned to our rooms to study, and I put him out of my mind. Why would such an attractive young man be interested in a girl like me? I was damaged goods, stripped of confidence.

Within fifteen minutes, there was a very gentle tap on my door. When it opened immediately, I turned to see him standing there with his twinkling, blue eyes, smiling in a way that would have melted the heart of Ivan the Terrible. I was shaking with excitement as he asked me to accompany him to the Bristol Old Vic' Theatre the following Wednesday. He backed out of the room, leaving the scent of Old Spice wafting on the air. It was a rare moment of pure bliss. I could not believe what had just occurred.

The first love of my life had a car—an ancient Morris, Series E—which meant that I could now see plays and films all the way through and still be home in time for curfew.

On our second date, we began to learn more about each other. When I told him that I lived on a small farm in Wales, he looked into my eyes and said earnestly,

"I have been looking for you my whole life."

I melted into his arms. I believe he thought that a student studying veterinary medicine and a girl who might have the ability to milk a cow, shear sheep and treat them for footrot were compatible. On our third date, he said,

"I really regretted saying that."

Hmm! I deduced that he was a young man with another side yet to be discovered.

Very soon, however, we declared our undying love for each other by exchanging our college scarves, the outward sign of commitment amongst students then. A veterinary school scarf ranked quite high, but the medical school scarf was considered to be the number one acquisition for which to strive. A few of my contemporaries had already achieved that goal.

So, began a round of evenings at the Bristol Old Vic' theatre or the cinema, dances at the Victoria Rooms in Bristol and wonderfully romantic occasions when, dressed to the nines in evening attire, we attended the Veterinary Students' Ball and the Barrow Ball.

My life had changed. Previously, my own perception of my character and my appearance had been eclipsed by so much internal torment—I had been made to feel ugly and worthless. John made me feel attractive and loved which boosted my confidence and began the healing of my bruised heart.

It was a long time before I felt comfortable enough to tell him anything about my family. He would, of course, never get to know all the gory details. I knew the day would come when he would ask me about my father. It was still so difficult for me to admit to anyone, even someone I loved deeply, that my parents were divorced.

Because of my grandmother's continued outbursts, my mother had moved back into the bungalow, so when John expressed an interest in meeting her, I reluctantly agreed to take him home.

Any apprehension that I had experienced on the journey to Wales dissipated immediately on our arrival. My mother was bowled over by John's charm. I had expected her to be daunted by his slick appearance, but he had such a natural way of putting women at ease. He made me feel comfortable in my own home for the first time in my life. He had helped me in surmounting my first hurdle—in lifting my burden a little.

Eventually, John invited me to meet his parents in Loughborough. They were delightful, working-class people but, on that first visit, I really began to understand the real John and how much we really did have in common.

We were both grappling between two classes of society, but tackling it in very different ways. Whereas I, because of my insecurity, shied away from contact with the upper-class, John had decided to bludgeon his way into it. He was determined to get ahead and ascend the ranks. He had the confidence to do so.

The country gentleman dress was all part of the act, and while I often found his behaviour embarrassing, I admired him enormously for his determination not to accept that he was in any way inferior because of a working-class background.

Unfortunately, although he was so adored by women, he did not relate well with his classmates. His behaviour isolated him. Most of the other students found him somewhat affected and derided him for aiming to be someone he was not. I wish they could have understood him as I was able to do.

One of his classmates, who also married a Barrow girl, seemed to have held a particularly strong aversion to him. At one of the reunions, when that particular gentleman asked me what on earth had attracted me to John, and why I had spent so many years of my life with him, I found myself vigorously defending him—attempting to explain how difficult life can be for those of us who have been educated beyond our class and how the British class-system can be so destructive.

In his country gentleman role, John invited me, and gradually a group of other veterinary students and girls from the college, to go Beagle hunting with the Clifton Harriers. This involved tearing through the countryside in hot pursuit of hares. Isn't it amazing to what lengths one is prepared to go for love? I can't say that I enjoyed the hunting, but I was grateful that the Beagles appeared to be far too slow to catch anything on the majority of occasions.

Following the hunt, there would be a delicious

spread in one of the large country mansions in the Somerset countryside which we would attend, although we hardly looked like dyed-in-the-wool hunting types. We were referred to, in rather derogatory terms, as "the girls from the college." John had the moxie to carry off the situation perfectly, chatting comfortably with all the "To the Manor Born" types with their plum-in-the-mouth accents. They tended to migrate only towards John, while the rest of us, the lumpen proletariat, skulked sheepishly around the food, avoiding conversation.

The hunts were important to John, so I was willing to put up with them just to be with him. He exchanged his tie for a cravat for those outings, and I can visualize him also in plus fours and carrying a shooting stick which was his style, but that may just have been a figment of my imagination.

We also went to all the horse trials and the Point to Point horse race meetings to mingle with the gentry. That was nothing new for me as the country peasants were also in the habit of attending Point to Points in rural Wales, the only difference being that we tended to mingle with the other peasants.

On one occasion, along with Margaret and Tom, we attended the Mendip Horse Trials. John turned up in a tweed flat cap—what was considered to be suitable casual countryside wear for upper-class country gentlemen. Along with this newly purchased acquisition, he wore his high leather boots, his best Harris tweed jacket, plus fours and cravat. This time, he was most definitely armed with a shooting stick on which he had amassed a collection of badges on silk cords. He decided that we were going into the Members and Owners enclosure, and he marched forth with his typical sense of entitlement. A policeman stopped him and asked to see his membership badge, at which point he rattled his shooting stick in the policeman's face shouting,

"Take your bloody pick, my man."

The policeman was so stunned that he backed off immediately and let us in, much to the embarrassment of the rest of us.

Because we were the first of the three year trained teachers, the academic demands were not exactly rigorous at Barrow. We did not know the meaning of overwork. Everything would have been perfect but for two regular weekly events.

On Tuesday mornings, the college principal, Miss Graham, a slight, grey haired aloof character who with a fixed stare could make one feel completely inadequate and shake violently at the knees, would arrive from the main campus at Fishponds, in full academic gown, to try to educate us with readings from Dante's *Divine Comedy*.

One would have thought that Dante's *Divine Comedy* was a work to which I could have related well. Hell? Purgatory? Paradise? It was the story of my life, but, although the lectures occurred every week, my knowledge of Dante remained scanty. A few of the more intellectual students helped by asking profound questions, so Miss Graham tended to focus on them, while the majority of us tried, unsuccessfully, to give the impression that we were enthralled.

On Thursdays, we travelled to Fishponds in Bristol for our special subject—the day on which the country cousins met the city girls who all seemed to be so much more sophisticated than us. We all hated that day, being cast out of the wonderfully protective environment of Barrow and bussed across the city to spend an entire day in what we considered to be a much inferior and soulless place. After a full day of lectures, we returned, exhausted, through the seamier parts of Bristol, in the rush hour, only just in time for high tea.

Beginning on Wednesday evenings, the Barrow sick bay would begin to fill, mainly with those sick only at the thought of what was in store the next day. I admit, once, to exaggerating an indisposition myself, and recall, on that occasion, Mrs. Gibbs's raised eyebrows as she entered the infirmary to find every bed full, and how she hurried to bring in Miss Jelley and Miss Andersen to witness the scene. We knew she wasn't fooled, but, as was her way, she turned a blind eye, smiled knowingly and continued to pamper us like deserving patients.

The other situation which was much worse than the weekly Thursday trauma was the annual teaching practice. The first one was following the Christmas or spring break, and I was so sickened by the thought of it that I tried to come up with a sure way to avoid it by not returning to college.

That was the only time that I had ever discussed my personal feelings with any member of my family, and, for some unknown reason, I confided in Aunt Blodwen that I had decided to leave college. She told me, in no uncertain terms, that there would be no unfinished business for me and managed to make me feel guilty enough to return. I was embarrassed, and angry with her, but, in the long run, I knew she had done me a great favour.

Prior to the teaching practices, we would spend much time preparing lessons and visual aids and collecting items of interest for the upcoming classes. One unforgettable item was a sheep's skull which Margaret thought would be a perfect teaching aid. No doubt it was, but the preparation left something to be desired. Tom had procured it from the anatomy department at the university but delivered it complete with the flesh still on it.

Margaret was not deterred by the woolly head or the doleful eyes. She threw it into a pot and boiled it in a mixture of Tide and bleach. For reasons known only to herself, she had chosen to do it on the night of the College Ball. The acrid smell of rotting meat mixed with

166

bleach that permeated throughout the building was so overwhelming that she was ordered to dispose of it without delay but, to her, it was of such value that she ignored the order and put it in a bucket hanging out of her bedroom window where, after several days, the smell eventually dissipated. The sheep's skull survived to excite a generation of small children in various parts of England and Canada.

Margaret and Tom Hurst dressed for Barrow Ball. Who knew a sheep's head hung from her window?

When the day of departure from the college to our assigned schools arrived, I can never forget the overwhelming apprehension I felt, as I boarded that bus along with the other girls who were dropped off in the far-flung corners of Somerset. A mixture of fear and homesickness for Barrow welled up in my throat as we stopped off at places like Shepton-Mallet, Midsomer-Norton and Chew-Magna. Some of the girls were lucky enough to be dropped off in pairs, but I was, again, taken alone to Glastonbury where I was housed with a religious family in a very austere home.

Every morning, I dawdled up the drab, mostly deserted street, past the Clarks' shoe factory, feeling utterly dejected, thinking that I would have been far happier working on the hardware counter at Woolworths and to hell with Miss Whatley and Miss Congleton.

The dread of the situation was minimal by comparison to the terror I felt at the thought of Miss Congleton arriving, unannounced, to observe me teach. During my pre-practice interview, she had kindly referred to me as a "shop girl," so presumably her expectations were not high.

When she finally came, I was out in the yard teaching physical education which had been so well set up by the classroom teacher that I looked like a professional.

Halfway through the lesson, I spied Miss Congleton peering menacingly through some branches on the other side of the school fence, but I managed to prevent my heart from beating right out of my chest, and I breathed in deeply. I seriously wondered if I could stage an Aunt Maisie-style faint.

After she had observed me interacting with the students inside the classroom, she left me a very nice note which, reading between the lines, told me that she had been pleasantly surprised by what she had observed.

A few students did not make the grade after that first practice, so our numbers began to dwindle. I was very glad to have got the first one successfully behind me. I reluctantly had to admit that the head of the family really had been right.

At the weekend, John came down to visit. I was

longing to see him, but I remember him arriving completely overdressed and how embarrassed I was that he sat in my host family's living room not realizing that his bow tie was attached only to one side of his collar. Everyone in the room was aware of it, but we carried on as if it was the latest fashion. How easy it would have been to have told him quietly to fix it in a way that would have been much less of an embarrassment, but, after all, we were British.

We went to Weymouth for the day and strolled along the beach—young lovers, holding hands—wasting most of our precious time together bemoaning the fact that we would not be able to see each other for two long weeks.

When the practice was over, with what ecstasy we returned to Barrow, to Miss Jelley, Miss Andersen and Mrs. Gibbs.

Thanks to John—a bull-shitter of the first order—who made such a fuss of first Treasure and then Lollipop, imparting 'expert' veterinary advice, even though he was only in his second year of study—I became a favourite of Miss Jelley. She found John absolutely enchanting, and I was the fortunate beneficiary. I felt that she was almost living vicariously through what she saw as a perfect relationship.

It wasn't perfect, of course, or even close. Just like all the other relationships that had formed over the year, the course of true love was running anything but smoothly:—slamming of car doors, raised voices over the phone, angry footsteps pounding through the halls, returning of scarves, words and letters of recrimination, floods of tears, broken hearts—it was all part of the student dating world.

At the end of the year, our second-year students left, and a new intake arrived in October. To make room for them, we had to be turned out to houses and farms in the neighbourhood. We were, by this time, disinclined to leave the comfort of the nest, and if I remember rightly, there were those amongst us who cleverly managed to invent valid sounding, though questionable, reasons why they should stay.

I was dispatched to Gable Farm, Wraxall, to the Davis family. My roommate, Chris Turner, had a reputation for wild behaviour. She had the audacity, between classes, to sneak off to Bristol on her scooter to drink coffee with young men who were considered to be beneath our social class. It was thought that I, in a stable relationship, could be a sobering influence on her which is why we were housed together. It was John's steadiness, rather than mine, perhaps, which was the deciding factor.

We spent most of that year fending off the advances of Mrs. Davis's son, John, and the hired help, Roger and Tim, as well as the savagery of the family dog which lay in wait for us at every turn and had a habit of sitting under the table and drawing blood from any foot that moved.

Another older lodger, a dour, humourless individual who worked for the local paper, was noticeably afraid of the dog so, inevitably, became the main target. He tried, in vain, to get Mrs. Davis to put the dog outside during meals, but she clearly liked the dog far more than the lodger which wasn't difficult.

One day, at the supper table, a discussion on running prowess took place and, for some bizarre reason, Mrs. Davis, who was a smart, sophisticated lady, challenged the lodger to a running race. They were both in their early fifties. We, in our late teens, thought it most ungainly and improper for people of that advanced age and mien to consider racing with each other, but the day was set, and we all went out to the field to witness the spectacle and cheer them on.

Mrs. Davis, for whom we were cheering, was well in the lead, when she suddenly stepped in a rabbit hole and down she went, breaking her arm. The cast served as an embarrassing reminder of her foolishness for the next six weeks. I could see that the lodger got some satisfaction from levelling out the score, even though the dog continued its relentless attack on his ankles.

Mrs. Davis was a friendly lady who bent over backwards to make us feel welcome, but we soon realized that her priority was to get her son married off to a college girl. She became quite hostile towards us when she saw that we were not going to capitulate to his advances. Even though John came to the farm often, and she could see that we were very committed to each other, she didn't accept that as a deterrent.

The two farm hands, Tim and Roger, were also determined to woo us. Roger invited us both to his twenty-first birthday celebration, deliberately excluding our partners. I was embarrassed by his attention to me and especially when he insisted on having me by his side to cut his birthday cake, as if I were the special girl in his life.

That night, we were long past our curfew returning to the farm. On our arrival, Mrs. Davis joked that the college had called to see if we had checked in on time. Chris was under a special curfew, because of further coffee drinking with boys who were considered inferior which my steadying influence had been unable to prevent. When she heard Mrs. Davis say there had been a call from the college, she didn't wait to question it but ran out of the house crying and hid. Mrs. Davis took the precaution of bringing her scooter into the living room to prevent a quick getaway.

We searched the farm for hours and finally found her sitting high up in an apple tree.

Since nothing could persuade her to descend, it was decided that Miss Andersen and Mrs. Gibbs should be brought down from the college to deal with the situation. Chris eventually climbed down from the tree, shaking with fright, to hear Miss Andersen state calmly, before returning to her car,

"Well, Miss Turner, it is a pity that you chose tonight for your little escapade, as it's early communion service tomorrow, and the clocks go forward tonight for the spring equinox," and, without further ado, she drove off into the night.

Poor Chris thought that she was off the hook and was greatly relieved, but she had been given one too many chances, and the next morning, her mother was called to take her home, bringing her future as a teacher to an abrupt end.

Years later, Mrs. Gibbs, giving an interview, related this story as one of the most memorable evenings of her career. Other memories she could also recall, but most of them, she said, were unsuitable to speak of, and she could be sued if she recounted them.

John was now studying at Langford in Somerset which was close to Barrow. He was in lodgings with a delightful couple who welcomed me into their home. We often had afternoon tea there and then headed over to Langford's common room to watch "That Was the Week That Was"—the first of the clever satirical sketches starring David Frost, Millicent Martin, Bernard Levin and others. It was immensely popular in England and ran for two seasons before being pulled before the 1964 general election.

I was once more without a room-mate, but the second-year teaching practice was looming ominously, and now that Chris had gone without my steadiness being able to salvage her future career, I was sent off to Wiveliscombe with another problem student, Anne Swiss.

She was an extraordinary girl who, though not exactly an oil painting, always had a list of suitors waiting in the wings. She could wrap men around her little finger.

For two years, she dated a delightful student who

hitchhiked every weekend all the way from Lampeter, in West Wales, to see her. That was no mean feat before the Severn Bridge was completed, linking England and Wales in 1966. She treated him like dirt, but he came dutifully every weekend until, finally, she cast him aside like a used rag.

Again, my steadying influence failed to help Anne. On our second day of practice, she was taking me to school on the back of her scooter when we hit a car and ended up in Taunton hospital. The following week, she insisted on riding her scooter to her birthday party in Plymouth. While returning to Wiveliscombe, she had a serious accident which finally persuaded her parents that the scooter had to go. She spent two days in the hospital and a further two days in bed at our digs crying out in pain from her injuries. She was unable to continue teaching and had to be returned to college. I was envious that she had found a way, although painful, to avoid teaching practice. I couldn't wait to get home to Barrow.

At the end of my second year, I agreed to go on a hitchhiking trip around Europe with Jan and another girl, Pauline Harper. John was very displeased, believing it to be highly risky, but apart from a few French men exposing themselves to us—thinking that we were prostitutes—and a group of Italians on a train, one of whom proposed to me, we came through the experience quite unscathed.

It was my first trip abroad, but we had so little money—not even enough to buy a camera between us— and we covered so many countries in such a brief time, that I remember little about it, other than being in St. Mark's Square in Venice on Easter Day which was a particularly moving experience and not easily forgotten.

On our return to college, the geography lecturer expected us to put on a presentation about our travels, but I am embarrassed to say that the only fact that was revealed was that our knowledge of European geography was still sadly lacking.

The workload at college seemed to be even less in the third year, and my clearest memories are of the Beatles bursting onto the music scene in 1962, of jiving to the music of Buddy Holly and dancing at the Vic' Rooms in Bristol, to the bands of Acker Bilk, Kenny Ball and Adge Cutler and the Wurzels. Then there was the Vets' Ball and the Barrow Ball for which we dressed up feeling just like Jane Austen characters in our romantic surroundings.

Money was short, so usually we spent hours, not studying, as we should have been, but making our own dresses for the balls. I remember an aqua-blue, velvet number that I made which, at the time, I thought was stunning, but I wonder what I would think of it now?

Mrs. Gibbs and Miss Jelley would always ask to see us before leaving for the balls so that they could check us over and ooh! and aah! just like loving parents.

Dressed in the aqua—blue, velvet number—John and I with Anne Swiss and David Bardsley

Our carefree world was upended abruptly in October of 1962, by the real threat of nuclear war. A heavy ceiling of gloom hung over us as we tried to come to terms with what we really believed could be the end of the world. We huddled together in silent groups, listening to every radio broadcast. We spoke of nothing else. Unbearable tension was felt everywhere.

A spy plane had discovered nuclear missile sites under construction by the Russians, in Cuba. President John Kennedy had ordered a naval blockade of Cuba. Thankfully, in late October, Nikita Khrushchev agreed to withdraw the missiles the following spring. It was the closest the world had come to a nuclear war.

"Ban the bomb" marches had occurred since 1958 when John Collins and Bertrand Russell founded the Campaign for Nuclear Disarmament—C.N.D. That was the birth of the emblem of the British anti-nuclear movement which has now become an international symbol for peace.

The last march from Trafalgar Square to Aldermaston, Berkshire, where the Atomic Weapons Research Establishment was located, took place in 1963, the same year the International Test Ban Treaty was signed, partially banning nuclear testing. Thousands of students were there in their duffel coats and black stockings. For the time being, we felt we could relax, but it had been a serious shake-up for many of us who had never really had to deal with the horrors of war as many of our parents and grandparents had done.

Christmas came, a particularly memorable time in the idyllic surroundings at Barrow with decorations adding to the beauty and elegance of the stately rooms. All the decorations were made by the students using natural materials from the countryside—greenery, dried flowers, pine cones, berries and branches.

I have never forgotten the art lecturer's scathing opinion of glitz and glitter. Visiting the malls of Vancouver today, I wonder what she would say? She would be glad to know that at least one of her students took her message to heart.

An unfortunate incident occurred one Christmas when the decorations were taken down and the greenery disposed of close to the fence separating the college grounds from a farmer's field. The cows consumed the yew branches which made many of them sick and caused the death of at least one of them. On our return to college in January, there was some explaining to do and compensation to be given to the farmer.

The third year flew by much too fast, and, other than the looming teaching practice, life was so good that we didn't look forward to the day when we would be cast out into the real world.

John and I, and Margaret and Tom who, despite the odd spat, seemed to be well on their way to wedded bliss, spent lots of time together going to films, the theatre, dances and, of course, the Saturday morning hunts and horse races.

The hunts followed the Saturday morning gardening sessions with Miss Jelley. I had had so much experience at Tregare school with Mr. Williams in my formative years that, again, I was one of her favourite students though I, like the others, spent a lot of time when out of her sight, giggling like a schoolgirl in the Shrubbery.

Ros, Margaret and I involved in some serious gardening and a little giggling

As we were coming to the end of the third year, John and I began to think of the future. He applied to a practice in Essex so I applied to a school there. We had never discussed marriage, but had comprehensively covered what breed of dog we might own in the years to come.

Set to begin my career, John's final results arrived and, to his dismay, he had failed a crucial part of the exam. The idea of moving to Essex by myself, after three highly social years at Barrow, was just too depressing, so I cancelled my contract and applied for a job in Bristol. In those days, one could put a pin on any town anywhere in England and be assured of a job there. Most people had arranged to go to other parts of England by then, so I knew that I would have to live in a flat by myself in Bristol.

In her Christmas letter of 2005, responding to my ramblings about college days, Margaret Perren, now Hurst for over 50 years, wrote,

"You do realize that this reminiscing is definitely a sign of our advancing years."

How true! More and more I find myself thinking back to what Margaret refers to as, "The Good Old Days."

George Bernard Shaw once said,

"Reminiscences make one so deliciously aged and sad."

Well, there's no doubt that I feel aged but not sad. When I think of that time that we all spent together at Barrow, I am replenished with a permeating warmth, that same warmth that nurtured us and surrounded us all those years ago.

Leaving home can be a very traumatic time for young people, but I felt as if I were leaving home for the first time when I had to leave Barrow Court, knowing that I could never return.

On the final day, I was so reluctant to tear myself away. I had experienced such happiness there. I had come far along a road that had once been so rough and stony. I wanted to savour those last moments—walk the panelled halls—wander the ornate gardens. I wanted to reminisce in the Shrubbery and the old Tithe Barn, reliving the romance, but I was robbed of those last, essential experiences by John who was in such a hurry to whisk me away to an exceedingly dull party in Loughborough where I knew no one.

I was so quiet on that journey. I felt such a mixture of anger, frustration and sadness. My years at Barrow were over and had been brought to such an abrupt end. I had to close a door firmly behind me to face the reality of a working life and an unknown future.

ROSE DUDLEY

CHAPTER FOURTEEN

"Children are like wet cement.
Whatever falls on them makes an impression"
Dr. Haim Ginnot

I shudder when I think back to how unprepared I was for the rigors of a classroom that was to be entirely my responsibility. As a student teacher, one can rely, in part, on the organization and the discipline of the classroom teacher. The real thing was similar to being cast out in a rough sea, in a rowboat without oars.

I was assigned to Blaise Infants' School in Henbury on the west side of Bristol. The city schools in the early sixties were considered very innovative and many of them had adopted the "Free Activity" method of teaching. A more appropriate term would have been the "Free for All" method.

The children were arranged in family groups, arriving in the term in which they turned five years of age and remaining with the same teacher for three years— tough on the children who ended up with a lousy teacher and vice versa.

I began with a class of 36 five to eight-year-olds in September which grew to 43 by the following March.

On the first morning, faced with a multitude of little people, some of whom had been in the classroom for two years and were, therefore, more knowledgeable about the system, I felt like a mother hen whose chicks had all hatched out at once or a frog surrounded by thousands of tadpoles darting around the pond hiding in every nook and cranny.

It's one thing to have a classroom teacher show you the ropes while you are a student, but to have a six-year-old telling you,

"No, Miss, we don't do it like that—no Miss, you have to collect the dinner money before you take the register—no, Miss, we don't make our eights like that, we make them like this," makes you feel like beating the little know-it-all over the head with a board eraser. Oh! there were no board erasers. Blackboards were too old fashioned for this school.

Basically, free activity meant that if a little girl wanted to spend the day in the play-house cooking plasticine rock cakes, I was not supposed to discourage her but perhaps suggest that she might want to weigh the ingredients—she invariably didn't—or if a boy was content to pour sand over his feet all day long, I could suggest that he see how many small cups it would take to cover his feet completely and what would be the equivalent in big cups.

It was all about discovery, but I had no way to monitor exactly what was being discovered except the certain discovery that I had entered the wrong profession. I was basically just a supervisor who fumbled my way through the days surrounded by a mass of pint-sized bodies scurrying from place to place around the room, making demands, talking all at once and firing questions at the speed of lightening.

There were no breaks other than a long one for lunch, as it was considered psychologically damaging to interrupt a child who might be creating a masterpiece in paint or clay or egg boxes. I was given short breaks to use the bathroom, when a teachers' aide would walk around to intercept any skirmishes that might occur, but, in truth, those were few and far between, as the children were very happy spending their days doing just what they chose to do.

Lesson planning was minimal as the ideas were supposed to come from the children, and I suppose a more experienced teacher would have been ready to cash in on any interest shown or expressed, but for the first year, I am sure that I missed golden opportunities to set children off on their life's path.

Any adding, subtracting, dividing or multiplying was learned without the use of symbols. I felt very insecure about that and one day gave the children a page of addition and subtraction. One would have thought I had committed a crime worthy of a gaol sentence. I was told in no uncertain terms, by the headmistress, that that was never to be done again.

I spent hours, one weekend, drawing pictures and printing letters to make a magnificent alphabet to display around the room, but when the head saw me proudly putting it up, she became almost hysterical and told me that I was not understanding the system. She was right on that score. My beautifully crafted alphabet was destined for the rubbish bin, while the children were expected to discover letter sequence by osmosis.

A very worrying part of my day was that if my students suddenly had a yen for making music they could leave the classroom and go off to the front hall where there was a huge selection of instruments to play, or if they didn't like any of those that were available to them—they invariably didn't—they could use the supply of old boxes, paper, paint, beans conkers, pine cones, glue and staples to make something more to their liking. Most of what they made was not at all to my liking nor was the mess that resulted.

They could also go to the gym or outside on the patio to play games or do some climbing or other exercise. Keeping track of them all was a nightmare, as they could easily have gone for a stroll across the Downs or gone home for that matter. I can't be sure that some did not. I was always trying to count them, but with 30 to 40 of them all moving around at once, it was impossible. I had to try not to worry about them, to accept the casual nature of the learning environment. No one else seemed at all concerned.

Adding to the overcrowding were busloads of teachers from other parts of the country who came in droves to see the new, innovative method of teaching. They went away enormously impressed but leaving us all exhausted.

The headmistress, Winnie Stevens, as cold a personality as Miss Graham, the college principal, was approaching the end of her career, so she spent most of her time hiding behind closed doors in her office keeping a low profile. She did, however, teach script writing to all the children towards the end of their third year, as well as ensure that they had mastered reading, which, by some miracle, they had. They were well prepared for the Junior School and, as far as I know, the teachers were always pleased with the new intake.

Somehow, I muddled my way through the first term, hoping that those imprints in cement were setting straight and true.

It was an age when teachers earned respect, and parents did not question their motives. Nowadays, teachers tend to be the enemy, and children are just puppets with parents pulling the strings. Nowadays, parents think they have far more knowledge than teachers, based purely on the fact that they were once in school themselves.

I was generally liked and trusted by the parents of my little charges even though I had failed them by demonstrating alphabet and number sequence, and I began to gain my confidence. I didn't panic if a child spent the whole week in the play-house cooking a birthday cake or another one decided that his new goal in life was to climb the 25-foot high climbing frame over the cement play area ten times a day. Miraculously, no one ever fell or got injured.

The rest of the staff were very supportive, and I became friends with all of them even though, at the time, I considered them to be quite ancient. When my future mother-in-law asked me about my colleagues, I told her that they were mostly older women in their thirties. That might have been the first strike against me. Actually, it wasn't. Worse was to come.

Joyce Davis, one of my colleagues, lived just around the corner from my flat in Cotham, so she agreed to drive me to school every day. She was some years older than me—a girl who was very comfortable in her single state. I would come to envy her that. She went home to Merthyr Tydfil to visit her parents most weekends, because she had no wish to participate in the social scene, such as it was.

I was a heavy sleeper in those days, and, often, I awoke to her frantic knocking on my door. Several times, I made her late for school and on the third occasion, Winnie called me into her office and gave me a severe dressing down. I was once more a defeated child standing before my grandmother—a life sentence.

I was long enough in the profession to see different approaches to teaching go around in circles. I think we may be back at the "Free Activity" method once again, but I was in and out of it at least three times during my career, and it has always been presented as the "new innovative approach."

No one can fully appreciate the level of patience it takes to cope with the constant demands of small children in a classroom. One of my colleagues, writing a Masters' thesis on her experiences as a teacher in an infants' school, spent five minutes in my classroom, one morning, recording all conversation, without my knowledge. She entitled it:

"Five Minutes in the Life of an Infants' Teacher on a Friday Morning."

What follows is an excerpt from a copy that I will always treasure:

Ian: "Have you seen the rubber (eraser) Miss Lynch?"

Philip: "Can I sharpen my pencil Miss Lynch?—he

don't work Miss Lynch."

Ian: "Miss Lynch, have you seen the rubber?"

Mark: "It's alright if I go to the toilet, en it Miss Lynch?"

Ian: "Miss Lynch, *please* have you seen the rubber?"

Mark: "I *really* wants to go to the toilet, Miss Lynch, I *really* does."

Miss Lynch: "*No*, Ian, I have *not* seen the rubber, and *yes*, Mark, you *may* go to the toilet, and you *don't* need to ask."

Miss Lynch: "Sit down Mark Alexander!"

Mark: "I can't Miss Lynch, I aint got no paper."

Miss Lynch: "Well I can soon remedy that, so don't look so pleased with yourself."

Carolyn: "Miss Crossland calls these things zib-zabs. Is they zib-zabs Miss Lynch?

Miss Lynch: "I haven't the faintest idea what zib-zabs are Carolyn."

Carolyn: "Well that's what Miss Crossland calls em."

Miss Lynch: "Well then, they must be zib-zabs."

Janet: "This word won't fit in 'ere, Miss Lynch."

Miss Lynch: "Well, start a new line, for goodness sake!"

Jayne: "I can't find the rubber."

Miss Lynch: "Ian, please give Jayne the rubber."

Ian: "I aint got no rubber, Miss Lynch."

Miss Lynch: "Well, what on earth *happened* to the rubber?" [Miss Lynch sighs.]

Patsy: "They're all broke, the pencils is all broke."

Jayne: "Our Mum let us put our own sugar in our tea last night."

Miss Lynch: "Did she? How lovely!" [Miss L not really listening]

Philip: "Gareth keeps saying bad words Miss Lynch."

Miss Lynch: "Such as?"
Philip: "Thick Bum"
Miss Lynch: "Don't be ridiculous and sit down."
Gwynneth: "Can I have a piece of paper to cut?"
Miss Lynch: Yes, of course"
Gwynneth: "Yes?"
Miss Lynch: "*Yes!*"
Gwynneth: "Can I have a pair of scissors as well?"
Miss Lynch: "Yes"
Gwynneth: "Yes?"
Miss Lynch: "Go away and sit down."
Arnold: "Can I have a pair of scissors too, Miss Lynch?"
Miss Lynch: "You do *not* have to ask me, Arnold."
Tim: "My Daddy aint got no teef—he talks funny, but Mummy, she got denshers."
Miss Lynch: "Daddy should get dentures, too, shouldn't he?"
Tim: "Yes, but he's afraid the man'll bite him."
Miss Lynch: "Is he really?" That's interesting." [Miss L not looking at all interested]
Arnold: "This is a cat in a shoe."
Philip: "It don't look like a cat to me."
Arnold: "Yes, it do."
Philip: "No it don't, it's scribble." [Arnold hits Philip across the face.]
Patsy: "Miss Lynch, Miss Lynch, Arnold just hit Philip across the face."
Miss Lynch: "Arnold, you know you shouldn't hit people in the face."
Arnold: "But, but, but…..."
Miss Lynch: "I know. Philip was being critical."
Kevin: "What's critical Miss Lynch?"
Miss Lynch: "Wait, I'm helping Anthony with money."
Anthony: "There, that's 13 pennies."
Miss Lynch: "You can't say 13 pennies, can you?"

Anthony: "No, you can say 13 pence".
Miss Lynch: "How many for a shilling?"
Anthony: "Eight?—Ten?—Six?"
Miss Lynch: "You're guessing, aren't you? Go and find out."
Tim: "I has to sleep with Mummy now."
Kim: "What about Daddy?"
Tim: "Oh! he sleeps downstairs now. Mummy don't want him in her bed no more."

Well, they say patience is a virtue, and I managed to develop it over time. I wasn't exactly in love with the idea of teaching for the rest of my life, but I had chosen my career, and changing professions just wasn't done as freely as it is done today. Besides that, I did not have a clue what else I was suited for, other than labouring, so I did the best job I could and expected that things would improve with experience. They did.

CHAPTER FIFTEEN

"You should celebrate the end of a love affair as they celebrate death in New Orleans, with songs, laughter, dancing and a lot of wine."
Francoise Sagan

I missed the social life at Barrow and the close friendship of girls my age. I was very lonely living alone, and John had to knuckle down to work in order to pass his exam so I did not see him often. Margaret and Tom still made up an occasional foursome and, at weekends, when Tom was ministering to the cat, dog, budgie and hamster population of Clevedon, Margaret came into Bristol where we shopped and treated ourselves to beans on toast in a restaurant. For one and sixpence, just cents, it was a bargain for poorly paid teachers.

Two other girls lived in the room next door, sharing a bathroom with me. Both, having recently broken up with boyfriends, had a rather dim view of men in general. One of my other college friends, Ros, who had also recently been abandoned by her college boyfriend, drove down from Berkshire to stay weekends and occasionally, I was drawn to go home by the same compulsion that had rendered my mother incapable of disentangling herself from those snarled roots. Distance can so easily blur reality.

But nothing had changed there and it never would. My grandmother was still regularly causing havoc and the family remained defenceless. As I had now partially graduated to the visitor category, I experienced a little more of "the sweetness and light" side of her split personality, but I was privy to the truth, so her duplicity angered me. Her continued castigation of members of her own family and our decent, hardworking neighbours disgusted me. In all the years I had lived with her, she had never uttered a good word about anyone.

My mother was always very happy to see me, but we had little to say to each other. Her life, much like Uncle Philip's, continued to remain a mystery to me. What did she do while I was away?—did she go out with men?—did she have any kind of social life? Why didn't I enquire? Why didn't she ask me about my life? How sad it is that we knew so little of each other, both appearing to be so uncaring.

Haydn, who was still rather slight, had embarked on a Charles Atlas course. Maybe he did have designs on girls and thought that he would be more attractive to them if he was muscular. To this end, he had built himself a magnificent gym in Park Wood, manufactured from logs. It was an extensive and very professional structure. The course also recommended drinking four pints of milk a day.

It worked surprisingly well, or perhaps it was from lifting those heavy logs into position, for, in no time at all, he became very muscular and began to look just like Atlas holding up the world on the Charles Atlas advertisement.

Years later, when he had given up on the course, the muscle turned to fat, and he became very overweight and diabetic amongst other things. Currently, where no one is expected to be responsible for his or her own questionable decisions, he could have sued Charles Atlas for millions.

Because John was still a student, we continued to have access to the Vic' Rooms so went to the dances— jiving and twisting to many of the famous groups of the day. If one loved pop music, Bristol was a good place to be in the sixties. Many famous groups came there in and around 1963—Freddie and The Dreamers, The Searchers, Billy J. Kramer and The Dakotas to name a few. Apart from Adge Cutler and the Wurzels and Acker Bilk who regularly played at the Vic' Rooms, Johnny Slade and the Vikings and Dean Prince and the Dukes also appeared there.

At half-term in November, I decided to go home for the holiday. It was a better option than spending a whole week in Bristol by myself. John pleaded with me to stay so that I could go to the Saturday night dance with him. I will never know what would have happened if I had finally agreed, but I do know what occurred because of my insistence that I go home to see my family.

I arrived in Tregare on a Friday night, the twenty-second of November, 1963, the day on which John Kennedy was assassinated by Lee Harvey Oswald in Dallas. The whole world was in shock. No one will ever forget what they were doing on that day, but, for me, the day would be, for many years, connected to other more personal memories.

By the following Monday, despondent over yet one more staged "suicide under the stairs," the can of rat poison being waggled under my nose and the awful realization that I no longer wanted to call Oakdale home, I decided to return to Bristol where I knew I was loved.

I cycled the mile to the telephone box to call John. It was a cool, grey evening, and darkness was approaching. There was the warm, homely smell of bonfires in the air and the rustling of birds, settling into their roosts for the night. I felt so light-hearted knowing how delighted John would be to learn that I had decided to return to Bristol earlier than planned.

Immediately he answered the phone, I sensed that something was wrong, and my heart missed a beat when he said that it would be unwise for me to return earlier. I pleaded with him to tell me what was amiss, but he insisted that he was not able to give me the reason over the phone.

I cycled home, my carefree mood now as dark as the night. I do not know what thoughts went through my head that week, but the constant churning in the pit of my stomach made me physically ill.

My mother must have sensed that something was wrong, but, of course, I did not tell her, and she would never have asked. I had an inkling that my relationship with John was somehow in jeopardy, but I could never have guessed the reason. We loved each other, we were committed to each other. John was everything to me— my best friend. How could anything ever change that?

On my return to Bristol, at the appointed hour, John arrived at the flat, beautifully turned out as one might turn up for a business meeting—knife-edged creases in his pants and a shine on his shoes that dazzled.

When I stepped forward to hug him, he recoiled as if I were a leper. He skirted around me into the flat and sat on a chair at the end of the bed. He had obviously prepared his speech well in advance, and he got straight to the point:

"My feelings for you have been changing for quite a while now," he said, "And on Saturday, at the dance, I met a girl with whom I have fallen in love."

Well, what was I supposed to say to that?

"Congratulations, I hope you will both be very happy?"

I felt as if I had been dropped from a height and smashed into millions of pieces on the cement below. He went on to tell me that she had fallen for him in the same way.

"She was crying in my arms the other night." he said callously.

My, how touching, I know that feeling.

Then, as if the knife hadn't been thrust in deep enough, he brought out a series of photographs of her in a bathing suit to show me. Now, is that not crass in the extreme? She was tanned and beautiful with a mop of dark curly hair. In a feeble attempt to retaliate, I told him that she looked like a half-caste. It was the best I could do in the circumstances. Did I have a little of my grandmother's racial prejudice in me after all?

With the nasty business cleared up so neatly and painlessly for him, he stood to go, saying in a rather business-like way,

"You are a very attractive girl; you will soon find someone else."

Oh, gee, thanks! Well, that is some consolation! How decent of you to say so.

"Well, I don't regret our relationship," I said in a reasonably cordial tone, as he was leaving, to which he responded with the final thrust of the knife,

"Well, I do."

I didn't plead or grovel. I knew it was over. I asked him to return letters I had written to him in the past week as soon as he received them, and that he did— unopened.

As I let him out, he skirted around me to avoid bodily contact and, with the briefest "Goodbye," he was gone from my life as rapidly as he had come into it three years earlier at Barrow. I never saw him again.

Whoever said "It is better to have loved and lost than to have never loved at all," clearly had never loved and lost. They can do what they like at funerals in New Orleans, but in Bristol, at the end of that love affair, there were no songs, laughter or drinking of wine, I can assure you.

I had spent a fair percentage of my life with a man who I loved and who I thought had loved me in return, but to whom I had become a total stranger in the course of one week. How is that possible? Ah! The inconstancy of man.

I was in a state of shock, but I never ever shed a single tear. As the song says, "Big Girls Don't Cry." My upbringing had shown me how to deal with emotion— bury the pain and bitterness in your heart and seal it tight in an impenetrable shell for ever. There is nothing that can better prepare one for a traumatic experience than being raised in the school of hard knocks. I knew I would survive.

I cannot pretend that the hurt was not excruciating and the loneliness almost impossible to bear. That recurring dream returned—I could not disassociate my thoughts from my earlier prediction—that disaster would strike—that my journey through life would be long and hard. In my unhappiness, I reflected on my childhood experiences and convinced myself that I would never find happiness—I was damaged goods.

Every morning, exhausted from a sleepless night, I lay awake at the crack of dawn, hearing a double-decker bus straining up Cotham Hill in low gear. For ever, I will associate that sound with abandonment. For years, afterwards, the anniversary of John Kennedy's death would consume me with such a feeling of personal loss.

Looking back, I realize that I had let John off the hook too easily. It would have made no difference to the end result, but if I had wailed and cried and thrown myself at his feet begging and pleading in a fit of passion, at least it would have caused him a little well-deserved discomfort. Why didn't I? Miss Whatley's words, once again, re-echo in my head.

Somehow, I managed to get myself to school on Monday morning. A roomful of 35 or so demanding children can soon take one's mind off one's personal problems. I managed to throw myself into my work.

On hearing the news, Tom and Margaret were as sad as I, but Tom did not express surprise. I think he had always believed that John could be a bit of a cad. For the time being, Tom and I were on the same page.

While writing of this experience in my memoir, on vacation with friends in Mexico, I asked them to suggest words that could describe the feeling of being jilted by a lover after three wonderful years together: emptiness? heartbreak? dejection? rejection? loss? anger? bereavement? They were all full of serious suggestions. My husband's contribution?

"I suppose pissed off wouldn't be appropriate for that kind of occasion, would it?" We all dissolved in fits of laughter. His sharp-witted comments on the irrationalities of life have become anecdotes communicated in his inimitable style to the delight of all who love him. As our children say,

"You can always count on Dad to see the funny side of what others might see as a humourless or even the most tragic of situations."

I watched him lying back on his lounger. His eyes were closed. Open on his chest, and largely unread, lay, *A People's History of the United States* by Howard Zinn. He hadn't changed a bit since the day that I had first met him. I laughed. He looked up at me and smiled. The warmth of that smile hung on the air between us—the smile that had captivated me more than fifty years ago.

Returning to Bristol after the Christmas break was not easy. A city in which I had spent the happiest years of my life had suddenly become alien—as bleak as the bitter winter that I knew I was about to face. Everything looked drab and depressing. The nakedness of the trees mirrored the bareness in my soul. I no longer wanted to be there. I wandered the streets, dejected and alone, hoping to catch a glimpse of John as he drove by. It was a useless exercise I knew, and yet, in my misery, I continued to do it because it gave me cold comfort. I wanted to escape, but the hard reality is that one can never escape from oneself. The pain consumes one's every waking hour. It cannot be cast off and discarded like an old cloak.

I had made a commitment to a class of small children to whom I had become very attached. I made my job my focus. I should have called Anne Swiss. She would have had the best advice on how to move forward. Not knowing where she was, I knew I had to begin to create another life for myself.

Back in Wales, I had become reacquainted with a Monmouth School boy from Raglan, Peter. I shouldn't say reacquainted because the staff at Monmouth School for Girls had always done their darndest never to let us become acquainted in the first place. It would be more accurate to state that I had observed Peter from what they would have considered to be a very safe distance.

He was working for Lever Brothers, based in Bristol. He became a great companion as well as my regular supplier of free soap products. Some years later, I would hear him laughingly recall,

"It was amazing what you could get in exchange for a free box of Persil."

At a jazz club in Bristol, I met a young man, Andrew, with whom I became very close friends and with an introduction to a young T.V. news anchor, Jon, I soon had a busy social life which helped to fill the time if not the void. Anne would have given her seal of approval and, no doubt, more unsolicited advice.

Andrew lived with three other students so there was always plenty of activity at their flat. Both he and Jon had girlfriends in other parts of England, so relationships with them had no strings attached. What surprised me, however, was that, although they were both in long term relationships, it was apparent that they were ready to hop into bed with any girl who was willing. My personal experiences, when shared with them, seemed to confirm in the minds of the two girls next door, that men were generally untrustworthy.

I was flattered when Peter invited me to his company's weekend conference in Torquay. As a student with limited funds, my experience of alcohol had been limited, but Peter was a man of the world and ordered me two stiff gins and tonic before we set forth.

The journey was a memorable one for both of us, but not in the way Peter might have hoped—a dirty weekend in Torquay.

He was very particular about his appearance, quite a natty dresser—lots of suede and leather—and he always smelled divinely of expensive aftershave. Alas!—not on that particular evening. We arrived in Torquay, both he and I completely dishevelled in a car in need of fumigation.

We had made no less than five stops en-route, so that I could vomit beside the road. It took me most of the next day to recover and a long while to salvage what remained of that relationship.

Peter eventually married and lives here in Vancouver. We have enjoyed occasional dinners with him and his wife Sue. When I recently brought up the subject of our disastrous weekend together, he claimed that he could not remember it. How can something be so clear in one person's mind but cannot be recalled at all in another's? I know that each time I pour a gin and tonic for a friend, the smell immediately activates the memory of that disastrous journey.

Andrew had a very convenient arrangement in Bristol, as Anne, his girlfriend, was teaching in London. During the school holidays, she came down to Bristol as I departed for Wales. His perfect plan came to a sorry end when, on one occasion, I decided to return early to surprise him, and I did, but not in the way that I had thought. Anne was in the kitchen. Although I had always known of her existence, it was obvious that she had not been made aware of mine. Andrew looked rather sheepish, but knowing how he operated, I realized that he would invent a very valid sounding story to placate Anne.

During the time that I was dating the T.V. anchor, he was writing articles on morality for *The Bristol Evening News*, the gist of which was that contrary to public opinion, girls were not willing to sleep with every man they met. Clearly, he had been busily testing the field while his future wife, Wendy, worked herself to death as a nurse in a Southampton hospital.

I was flattered to be at least a part of the inspiration for the articles, but I was becoming increasingly wary of all men. I had been hurt so badly that it was going to take me a very long time to recover my trust.

Despite my unintended meeting with Anne, Andrew and I continued our friendship. He loved modern jazz which I did not, but if I could chase after hares and go to horse races accompanying a man in a flat cap and plus fours wielding a shooting stick, tolerating jazz clubs for Andrew's sake wasn't exactly a tall order. I didn't much like his motorbike, but at weekends, I risked my life going for long rides into the Somerset countryside.

In the future, the motorbike would drastically change Andrew's life. A year before my husband and I visited him in New Zealand, he had been hit by a driver skipping a red light. One of his feet was all but severed. Being such a keen outdoorsman, this must have been a devastating blow to him, but he seemed to have accepted his fate, with good grace, and was still managing to lead an adventurous life despite his limitations. We had travelled to New Zealand to hike some of the well-known trails. How he would have loved to join us! Sadly, his hiking days are over.

He was just as confused over his personal life. He was long divorced from Anne, had remarried, and then, in the process of a second separation, had taken up residence in a room in Anne's house, unknown, of course, to wife number two. I had sent cards to him and Anne every Christmas since they had moved to New Zealand, but I discovered, on that trip, that Anne had never seen one of them.

Anxious to leave a flat with such heart-breaking memories, I acquired a new room- mate and moved to rooms in Redland. I cannot remember one thing about the room- mate—not even her name—except that we had an unfortunate incident involving her pet budgerigar.

She asked me to cut its toenails. When she learned that I was a farm girl from Wales she possibly thought I had some previous experience. I had not. With the first snip, the unfortunate thing croaked in her hand. She never recovered from the shock. Immediately after we had committed the remains of the bird to the back garden, we parted ways.

Living alone would be more expensive, but as I did not have an option, I rented an apartment in an old house in Clifton in preparation for my return to Bristol after the summer holidays. The idea of living alone again rekindled all those painful memories.

Not having any plans for the summer and still feeling more than a little marooned, I decided to tag along with my old college friend, Ros, who, with two other girls, was taking her father's car and caravan to Spain.

On the day before our departure, one of the Barrow girls, Bobby, married her college boyfriend, Alan, in Weston-Super-Mare. Amongst the guests was Anne Swiss. Her former boyfriend, David, of hitchhiking from Lampeter to Bristol fame, had been invited, but she had decided not to tell him so that she could be free to play the field at the wedding. I have no doubt that she had given her address, as well as her vital statistics, to several men before we left the reception.

She gave me a lift to Berkshire, shocking me with stories of her escapades since leaving college. I recognized that her method of dealing with men, although callous, had been much more effective than mine.

As Ros and I and her two friends, Rosemary and Jen, set off for Dover the next morning, the three of them were in high spirits, believing that four young, unattached girls would probably attract a little attention on the beaches of Spain. I, with much less enthusiasm, tried to embrace the idea of a new adventure.

CHAPTER SIXTEEN

"True love is finding your soulmate in your best friend."
Faye Hall

I had left Bristol with mixed emotions. It had become a place associated with loneliness and heartache, but I still clung desperately to the past—for the city that had held such happy memories—for the city that had supported me along a healing path before abandoning me.

We girls spent a week travelling down through France until we arrived on a campsite in Santander, Northern Spain. There, we settled in for a week, our caravan right on the beach.

We were all sun worshippers, and in those days, long before the skin cancer scare, we lay out all day, without any protection, until we were as dark as the natives. How we all regret that, now that our skin is as wrinkled as prunes and tough as old boot leather.

As I watch all these nubile young girls on the beach here in Mexico, lying out in the tropical sun for hours at a time, I want to show them where it leads, but no one could have persuaded me in my youth that a dark tan was not attractive.

We whiled away our days sunbathing, swimming and reading. It had been only nine months since my traumatic break-up, but the memory of my former love was fading quickly in the Spanish sun.

When I thought of John, I saw him only in the context of Barrow Court and wondered how much that special place had nurtured our relationship, and what shreds remained of it once the curtains had closed on that romantic backdrop. Analyzing the relationship, I began to ask myself if we had ever really loved each other as we thought. What is love anyway and how does one ever know when one has found true love?

I believe our relationship had turned into a

comfortable, convenient habit. We had stopped valuing the small details of each other's lives, and I hadn't noticed that our life lacked intimacy. What I did remember was that John had become increasingly critical of my dress and my appearance. Had he realized that I was not the right person to accompany him on his climb up to the next rung of the social ladder? I had chosen to ignore the signs.

Having spent a few weeks in Santander, we moved to a campsite in San Sebastian. The day after we arrived, the weather began to change, and, by Sunday morning, the rain was coming down in sheets. This was not what we were expecting.

We sat around, moping all morning, while the rain poured down in torrents, bouncing like marbles on the roof of the caravan and cascading down the windows obscuring, in part, the view of the ocean which was, by then, a grey monstrous mountain of waves. Lakes had formed all around the campsite. Bedraggled campers waded through deep pools in rubber boots or flip-flops, making countless trips to the store or the laundromat purely to relieve the monotony.

We girls, unable to spend the day at the beach, had become restless and bored and were beginning to get edgy with each other in the confined space, and Jen, who was entering the record phase of an ailment—she had not had a bowel movement for fourteen days—was feeling decidedly uncomfortable and under the weather. Following our advice, she had been consuming about four kilograms of fruit each day, and we were all becoming increasingly concerned about its whereabouts.

Early in the afternoon, a young man with a round, ruddy face, piercing blue eyes, a cheeky smile and an unruly mop of strawberry blonde hair, peered through the window. Cheerfully, he asked where we were from. He had recognized our license plate as one from his home county in England.

We did not know at the time, but he had told his two friends with whom he was camping, that he would go off in search of some English "birds." He was looking especially pleased with himself on realizing that he had discovered the mother lode. We invited him in, but, first, he went back to look for his friends and within a few minutes, drenched and cold, they stepped into the caravan.

William, the tousle-haired one, was clearly the extrovert in the group. Peter was quiet and somewhat aloof which made him appear a little arrogant, but the one who immediately won the hearts of all of us was John, the quiet one with the shy smile.

He was the colour of burnt cinnamon, had dark curly hair, merry, grey eyes an irresistible smile and even teeth. Nice, even teeth have always been a must for me, as I come from a family who, like most Brits, have mouths that resemble Stonehenge. It is said that you can tell an Englishman as soon as he opens his mouth. Not many people realize that it refers to the teeth rather than the accent.

I loved the sound of his voice. It was not possible to tell from what area of England he had come. I recognized that he must have had elocution lessons too. He had an innocence about him which was so appealing. I would soon discover that it was a feigned innocence. As a naval officer, he had been around the block a few times. I had no idea, at that point, just how many times.

As he lowered himself onto the bench, he sat on a rubber cushion which squeaked. This seemed to amuse the child within him, and he continued to make the cushion squeak throughout the afternoon, laughing engagingly as he did so, causing us all to laugh with him. I was utterly charmed.

Is there really such a thing as love at first sight twice in a lifetime?

After an afternoon of lively conversation and

copious cups of tea, our new friends left to find a sheltered spot for their tent and arranged to meet us at the bull ring that afternoon—I can't believe that I agreed to that—and at the beach the following day, if the storm had passed.

Outside the bullring—left to right—William, Jen, Ros, Rosemary me and John

As they left, my eyes met John's, and I felt a warmth penetrate my whole being. Did I dare to hope that he liked me too? Too soon, the old doubts resurfaced, and that lack of self-esteem reared its ugly head. I had been in this position before.

At the beach the next day, we behaved as young girls normally do—vying for the boys' attention—wondering who might possibly form a relationship. It was obvious that we were all attracted to John.

We learned that he was in the Merchant Navy—hence the beautiful tan. William, the cheeky one, was studying medicine in London and Peter, the cool customer, was working in the world of finance.

John was reading Joseph Heller's *Catch 22*, a recently published, satirical, anti-war story the premise of which, simply put, is, if you were sane you had to fly combat missions in WWII, but if you were insane you had to prove it to be exonerated. If you were trying to prove that you were insane, it proved that you were sane—hence the catch.

The satire was lost on the average reader including me. It had attracted a cult following of young intellectuals and would eventually be considered one of the greatest American novels of the twentieth century. I suspected that my new love might be a pretentious book snob. Was I ready for that?

John was also studying for his Second Mate's certificate. We lay close to each other on the warm sand. I felt the electricity running through my body. I was conscious that he was feeling it too. I helped him with the memorization of the marine rules of the road. I found that I was far better at remembering them than he was. I can still recite, "When two power driven vessels are meeting end on or nearly end on so as to avoid risk of collision, each shall alter her course to starboard so as to pass on the port side of the other." If only I could now delete that useless information from my brain to make room for what needs to be there.

I also discovered that John was besotted with South America and had a whole library of books on the subject. He had been to South America on his travels and told me that he hoped, one day, to live there. He was learning Spanish in preparation for the move and had already memorized a useless lesson on the purchase of a red handbag. I don't think he told me, at the time, that he had been engaged to a girl—Eliana, from Valparaiso. He had eventually plucked up enough courage to tell his mother that news, which caused her to recoil in horror and question fearfully,

"Oh, my God! She's not black, is she?"

He was presently dating a girl from Peru by the name of Marianella. Good Lord! He was only twenty-one and had already had a lifetime of experience. I was unused to such worldliness.

That long-distance relationship, by the way, would cause him more than a little anxiety when he received a letter from his new girlfriend's mother asking him exactly what his intentions were with regard to her daughter.

That evening, in a nightclub, we danced to that wonderfully romantic Italian song:

"No, Ho, L'eta Per Amarti"—the Eurovision Song Contest winner of 1964 sung by Gigliola Cinquetti that was being played constantly in every bar throughout Europe that summer.

We were shy with each other, at first, but gradually we began to feel as if we had known each other for ever. We did not return to the table for the whole evening but danced away the night content in each other's company and oblivious to our friends.

Returning to the campsite, John pulled me aside and together, holding hands, we strolled up the hill behind. There, we sat on a grassy bank overlooking the campsite and the twinkling lights of the city of San Sebastian beyond. Crickets chirped loudly around us, happy that the balmy August weather had returned. We talked long into the night until the last camper's light had been extinguished and that first pink ribbon of dawn appeared in the eastern sky. It was a night I would remember for ever.

As we left the following morning, John came to say, "Goodbye." We exchanged contact information, and he asked if he could take my photograph. We stood there awkwardly for what seemed minutes, and then he stepped forward and hugged me close. I clung to him, not wanting to let go.

The picture that John took as we parted ways, I thought for ever.

"I'll never forget you," he said. I saw the sadness in his eyes. I could not fight back my tears. "I'll write," he added, and then he was gone.

I let the tears flow freely as we pulled away from the campsite heading homeward. Had it just been a bittersweet holiday romance or could this wonderful man be the mender of my broken heart? We had exchanged addresses, and he had promised to write, but I did not expect to hear from him again. I no longer had expectations as far as men were concerned.

Setting out on our return trip to Calais, everyone seemed despondent and unusually quiet. We had had no reason to leave San Sebastian in such a hurry, and it seemed pointless when we drove only a few miles to Biarritz in southern France and spent a day on the beach by ourselves. We had nothing to say to each other, and I was seething inside.

I returned to Wales in low spirits. All the songs of that time spoke of love:—"Can't buy me Love" by the Beatles, "World Without Love" by Peter and Gordon, "Don't Throw Away your Love" by the Searchers. I tried to ignore Roy Orbison's, "It's Over."

Much was my joy, when only a few days after I returned to Wales, John wrote to invite me to meet his parents in Henley-on-Thames. As it turned out, his parents were not prepared to welcome another of his girlfriends so soon after recovering from the shock of a possible Chilean daughter-in-law, black or otherwise, so I invited him to my house instead—a sign that I was maturing—realizing that I was not going to be judged by my surroundings or my past.

I had told him that I lived on a small farm in Wales, and he later admitted that he thought I was being modest. He believed he was on to a good thing—a wealthy farmer's daughter. When he arrived, he could see that I had been exaggerating, but, by that time, it was too late for him to beat a hasty retreat.

I had never spoken to my mother about my break-up with the first John, and she had never asked, but she happily welcomed my new love. She liked him immediately. Who couldn't? All women found him to be incredibly appealing. I seemed destined to fall in love with men who other women loved.

On meeting my mother, he commented,

"She's in such good shape for her age." She was only 42 years old at the time.

On meeting my grandmother, he was quite taken with her charm and how she laughingly explained the reason for the holes in her red Wellington boots. It would be some time before I would tell him the truth, and he would never witness the real person that she was.

For a couple of days, I showed him the sights, such as Tregare had to offer:—my old school, Park Lane,

Marble Hall, and, in typical Welsh fashion, the graveyard, resting place of my grandfather and Mr. Jenkins, and all those killed in tragic accidents, until he came down with a stomach ailment which he had obviously picked up in Spain.

While we were sleeping on the first night, I heard the heavy handle on the Aga door being lifted, the living room door handle turning and footsteps padding across the living room floor.

I lay there rigid in my bed, and then, in a panic, ran into John's room to alert him. We exchanged beds, but a little later, he also heard the strange noises, which made him feel exceedingly uneasy.

The next morning, when my mother started on her hair-raising ghost stories, he was quite ready to believe that he had been visited by a poltergeist. On visiting the local doctor, he told him that he felt he had been made sick by a ghost—was it "Ol' Robinson" up to his old tricks yet again? We had never known Mr. Robinson to be a malevolent sort.

We were both shocked by some of my mother's stories. She told us of a night when she awoke suddenly to find all the lights on and the doors wide open. When we asked what she had done on finding that, she responded, in quite a matter of fact way,

"Well, what do you think I did? I put out the lights, locked the doors and went back to bed."

John couldn't believe that she could be so calm about the situation. He wanted to leave at the earliest opportunity. We decided to go to Devon, leaving my mother to deal with the ghosts of Mr. Robinson and his bevy of supernatural friends. Mysteriously, as soon as we were out of sight of my house, John made a miraculous recovery.

Even more mysterious is that neither of us, now, has any memory of what exactly happened following the miraculous recovery, where in Devon we went or what we did when we got there. John has ransacked the house, searching for a trigger:—a photograph, a journal, our old love letters, his ship's log, anything—but all in vain.

Memory is so fickle. Why does the humiliation of poor Raymond Gwilliam come to mind, seventy years on, but the slate is blank for a time that John and I were all starry eyed and in love? Oh! if only we could all relive those moments of such tenderness and passion before we "have shuffled off this mortal coil."

At the end of the summer vacation, I returned to Bristol, to my new flat with an impressive name—No. 1 Westbourne Villas—off St. Paul's road in Clifton. The name was the only impressive thing about it. It was a dingy room on the top floor with a separate kitchen which also served as the bathroom.

An older man, Frank, and I shared the toilet on the landing. Since he was British also, Frank and I, with furtive movements, managed to avoid the embarrassment of arriving at the toilet at the same time, for the entire year that I lived there. I don't remember who replaced the toilet paper or which one of us cleaned the toilet, but I am sure that it was not a subject that Frank and I ever discussed.

The flat was advertised as furnished; it contained one soiled Victorian armchair, a bookcase, a boarded-up fireplace and a narrow, well-used bed with springs that had pierced the mattress.

When I complained about the state of the mattress to the old lady living on the floor below, she snickered,

"If that bed could talk, you wouldn't believe your ears, dearie."

I felt a little uncomfortable knowing that the bed might have a few more stories to tell in the not too distant future.

Up until December John was in London taking his Second Mate's certificate and on weekends he took the train down to visit me.

His mother was very strict and worried that she might become a grandmother sooner than she wished. For all she knew, she was already grandmother to several bambinos toddling around South America. We did not know why she was so paranoid, but, in the future, we would understand her concern and have enormous sympathy for her.

"I know you are going down to Bristol to sleep with that girl," she would accuse John, but he always assured her that he was staying with a friend.

Eventually, when the threat of a potential, black Chilean daughter-in-law had passed, John's parents invited me to Henley. His mother, Molly, made no bones about the fact that she was disappointed in his choice. She told him that she had always thought he would choose someone who was "tall and sophisticated." There was no getting around the truth that I was short and unsophisticated. What was even worse, I was Welsh! Welsh people were foreigners as far as she was concerned—not quite as foreign as Chileans, but foreigners nevertheless. She used to commiserate with her friend whose daughter had married a Spaniard:

"Why couldn't our children have chosen nice, refined English partners?"

The clincher came, only a few years later. Her daughter began dating a delightful Welshman—Lyndon Owen—who, by coincidence, came from Monmouthshire, too—close to Aberfan where, in October of 1966, the catastrophic collapse of a coal tip would snuff out the lives of 116 little children and 28 adults.

Sue, John's sister, had met Lyndon—always known as Lyn—at St. Matthias, my old college which by that time was admitting men. He told me that he fancied her as soon as he saw her in one of those dance outfits. Those dreadful coloured bloomers were not enough to curtail his passion, which proves, without a shadow of doubt, that there is no accounting for taste, and beauty does, indeed, lie in the eye of the beholder.

Molly seemed much more accepting of Lyn, even though he was a "foreigner." and exceedingly short, which many Welsh men tend to be. I believe she was completely bowled over by his charm and his voice; his lovely Welsh lilt was not unlike that of Richard Burton's.

I soon learned that one of the most notable peculiarities about the Dudley family was how the dinner table conversation always revolved around lavatories and the various goings on therein. All other discussions would ultimately revert to their favourite topic.

I had not yet met Great Aunt Esme, but an inordinate amount of time was taken up discussing her problem with constipation which seemed to affect the family's visiting schedule. She was unable to receive guests on a Wednesday because, I was told, it was her "go" day. I had never realized, until then, what a spellbinding subject bodily functions could be.

In future years, walking the "Coast to Coast" path in England with our friends, John and Chris and Herb and Penny, John was thrilled to discover, in the middle of a field, a flush toilet called, "The Dudley Elite." Imagine the excitement that was generated in the family over that piece of information. It only needed for them to discover, in the future, that they were distant relatives of Thomas Crapper to make their lives complete.

John's mother, Molly, spent a small fortune on clothes and shoes and was always very smartly dressed, but hardly what one would have called sophisticated herself. She was a stern looking woman with prematurely snow white hair—the result, I was told, of raising a son who, as a small child, refused to eat.

She fawned over him and made no bones about the fact that he was number one. His grandparents had also done the same, so I was surprised that his sister was so tolerant of the situation and is very close to him despite it. Together, we have always jokingly referred to him as "Molly's wonderful son."

John's Dad, Harold, was a gentle soul who was very welcoming. He was a tiny man with a noticeable limp which necessitated him walking with a stick. He tended to fall over a lot but received little sympathy from the rest of the family. The usual response, as everyone walked on ahead was,

"Oh! Harold! What are you doing down there? Get up for God's sake!"

He had been born with a dislocated hip which had never been treated. He weighed exactly eight English stones—112 pounds, in his overcoat. He joked that he had never had the courage to weigh while not wearing it. I could pick him up easily and carry him on my back which I frequently did for a lark.

Molly was a wonderful cook, but Harold was hardly the best advertisement for her culinary prowess. She loved to bake, and her three-tiered cake tin, always filled in all three tiers, became famous through two generations.

In later years, she did much of the baking for the tea shops in Henley, so if you ever travelled in those parts and had the luck to drop into "The Copper Kettle," you may well have sampled Molly's delicious baked goods.

John's sister, Sue, was just sixteen years old when I met her, and, like John, was not as innocent as her mother would have hoped. She was an attractive, dark-haired girl who looked remarkably like her older brother. She had already amassed a long queue of admirers.

The family was quite unlike mine in that they hugged each other often; it was obvious that John and Sue had been brought up in a very loving and respectful environment. I was very impressed that John's father always did the washing up after Sunday lunch and cleaned the stove inside and out while his mum had a rest in the sitting room. He also cleaned everyone's shoes, including mine when I was visiting.

In Wales, those chores were considered women's work. Welsh men, in general, were completely inadequate in the home. Most of them couldn't even make a cup of tea, and what was worse, they were not expected to. When I told Aunt Phyllis that John and his father participated in the household chores, she responded, referring to her husband and son,

"But these are *real* men."

John's father smoked a pipe, so the house always had such a warm, comforting smell of pipe tobacco. I took a tin of St. Bruno Flake for him on my visits, not realizing that each package was contributing another nail to his coffin.

Because Henley was where he had attended Grammar school, John had many former school friends in the area. We frequently met at "The Rainbow" in Assendon, the favourite local pub which belonged to the parents of one of the group, Roger Barefield. It was one big social scene with lots of drinking. I shudder to think how irresponsible the boys were in those days—drinking all evening, and then piling into cars to drive on to the designated party house. We managed to get as many as eight of us into William's MGB, and I well remember the night John, who had consumed far too many beers, drove his father's car right through the back wall of the garage into the garden.

Often the parties were at William's house by the river in Goring. His parents were very liberal in their acceptance of all his friends who were always welcome to help themselves from the bar.

We used to play a very childish game called "Tap, Tap" in which participants had to remove an article of clothing each time they couldn't come up with a correct answer between the taps. The boys' plan, obviously, was to get the girls stripped naked, but it always ended up the other way around.

After "Tap, Tap," we would raid the fridge and cook up a huge breakfast of eggs, bacon, sausage, baked beans and fried bread and then eat any left-over rice pudding before returning home in the early hours of the morning.

Tap, Tap in Goring, (left to right) Tub, Will, Helen, John, (naked) and Lee, (disgusted)

It makes me cringe to remember how we behaved. Imagine if our children had known about our complete lack of responsibility as they were going through their teen years? So frequently, we hear criticism of the younger generation, but I would be the first to admit that our children were far more responsible than we were at that stage of our lives.

On his visits to Bristol, John would arrive on a Friday evening and return to classes on the first train on Monday morning. I preferred spending the weekends in Henley as, with the departure of the first John, I no longer had a network of friends in Bristol, but the downside was that in Henley, we had Molly watching our every move like a hawk.

On an extended period between classes, John redecorated the flat for me. From a dingy, depressing place, with a few rolls of yellow wallpaper, he transformed the living room into bright and inviting living quarters. Once I had recovered the old chair the place began to live up to its name.

The kitchen was more of a challenge to modernize because of the bathtub which took up most of the floor space. It was porcelain—a quantum leap from the galvanized tin one at Oakdale—but it was covered by a hinged slab of plywood that acted as the kitchen counter when the tub was not in use. Taking a bath, therefore, necessitated the use of one hand to hold up the heavy slab of wood—hardly relaxing. On more than one occasion, the heavy lid fell on top of me when my arm got tired. Still, it was the Ritz compared to Tregare.

Since I had moved into the flat in September when the weather was still quite balmy, I hadn't noticed that there was no form of heating—not even one of those metered gas fires that need to be constantly fed with coins and always run out of gas when you don't have a shilling handy.

In a letter that I wrote to John after he had left that winter, I described the conditions:

"It is bitterly cold here tonight, the temperature in the flat is below freezing. The water in a bowl in the sink is covered in a thick layer of ice. In the mornings, I can hardly dress because my fingers are numb with the cold. I need to put my hands under the hot-plate to prevent frostbite. The landlady splashed out on an oil heater which I turn to its highest setting and bring right up against the bed. I am going to invest in some heavy flannelette pyjamas and a hot water bottle, otherwise I shall make history by being the first person to freeze to death in bed."

The rent for this freezer compartment was the princely sum of three guineas—about $8.00 a week and not exactly a bargain in 1964, and since I was only grossing £60—approximately $145 a month at that stage, I wasn't exactly flush with money. I always seemed to be in the red before the end of the month.

I was embarrassed when I went, with John, to the bank to draw out funds, and the teller told me that the bank manager had requested to see me the very next time I came in. He gave me a severe lecture, in which he explained to me that I could not continue to be so irresponsible, living beyond my means. I was £3—the equivalent of $7.00—overdrawn at the time. John, who has always had an incredible ability to handle money, has never let me forget that incident.

Now, in my second year at Blaise I, at least, had the advantage of being more experienced than two thirds of the children in the running of the classroom. I felt that I had a handle on things and when the busloads of teachers arrived, as they continued to do, I enjoyed pointing out all the advantages of the innovative system. They were all highly impressed, returning immediately to their own schools to adopt the same system there. Soon a large proportion of the children in English schools were making plasticine cakes in the play-house all day long, and everyone seemed to be immensely happy, until it became apparent that eighteen-year-olds were entering university without the ability to spell or write a grammatically correct sentence.

John's time in England came to an end on the completion of his Second Mate's certificate. He joined a ship leaving for North and South America, just before Christmas, and did not return for three long months—an eternity to me. He left me with just a photograph.

John at twenty - three—photograph taken by his father

And I gave him this one, recalling his penchant for South American chicas.

He had, and still has, a great love of Gershwin's "Rhapsody in Blue" which he always made a point of playing the day before his departure. To this day, when I hear it, I am filled with melancholy. To me, that music will always be associated with departure, absence and loneliness.

For me, personally, 1964 had been memorable. I had met the man of my dreams which had changed my mind about college days being the happiest days of my life.

It was a memorable year all round. It was the year that the Beatles had taken America by storm, and Beatlemania had gone into overdrive. With the Rolling Stones and the Animals in England and the Supremes and Bob Dylan in North America, 1964 was declared one of the greatest years for music in the last century.

It was also the year that the French and the English made a commitment to build a tunnel under the English Channel, linking the two countries, although it would take thirty years before it would become a reality. Naturally, there were many Brits who were terrified that their culture would be watered down by allowing the French such easy access to their island realm. My grandmother, not surprisingly, had much to say on the subject:

"Why in ell's name do we want those stinkin' ol' Frogs comin' 'ere when they can't even talk English? Let 'em stay in their own bloody country where they belongs, I says."

In America, Lyndon B Johnson signed the long overdue Civil Rights Act, and in 1964, for those who might be interested, Cassius Clay won the Heavyweight Boxing Championship knocking out Sonny Liston. Meanwhile, at Oakdale, my grandmother was continuing to throw knockout punches and winning every round.

Back in Wales, for want of something better to do, I continued to do the rounds of the Young Farmers' dances with Edwin, Tony and other local boys. Now that

John was in my life, Edwin was relegated to the transportation without any favours category, but he was a good sport about it and continued to be my chauffeur without any expectations, while I was spared the cowshed, stale milk and Brylcream odours that had not been a part of my life since Old Spice had taken their place.

Haydn and I spent a lot of time with Aunt Marion reminiscing about the past. Aunt Marion was the only member of the family who, in her later years, opened up about her childhood. Heartbreakingly, my grandmother had been far harder on her children than she had ever been on us.

Marion told us a story about when she, at age three, was given the task of watching to make sure that the crows did not carry off the new-born chicks. Being forced to sit for hours in the hot sun, she had fallen asleep and failed to see a crow come swooping down to take one of the chicks. For her inattention, she had been given a sound beating and threatened with the carving knife through the bars of a rocking chair. She has never forgotten it. In her nineties, she still suffers such profound anger and resentment.

Because of her upbringing, she, more so than the others, does not have a shred of confidence and yet, her personality, even in her old age continues, in small ways, to resemble her mother's. We pitied her husband, Lewis, who was a quiet, gentle man, much like my grandfather, but we have always been able to rib Aunt Marion about the way she treated Lewis. Sometimes, my husband tells me that I am getting more like Aunt Marion every day. Can one ever cast off the tainted clothing of one's environment—or could it be heredity?

Marion and her sisters and brother never seemed to recover from those early jealousies that had been caused by their mother's unfair treatment of them. I vowed that when I had children I would treat them all exactly alike, and make sure that they grew up loving each other.

On a lengthy visit to Canada shortly before her death, Aunt Blodwen spent much of her holiday criticizing first one of her sisters and then another. She appeared only to favour my adopted cousin, Paul, who was a complete no-good as it transpired. Aunt Blodwen, like my mother, had an unfortunate habit of propping up lost causes.

Finally, in exasperation, I responded to my aunt's criticisms,

"What a pity it is that all of you sisters appear to hate each other so much. Why do you continue to let your mother psychologically manipulate you from the grave? It was always in her best interest to tear you apart, and you fell for it every time. Now she's gone. You don't have to hate anymore."

The shock on her face from being challenged, with such honesty, was palpable. She never again said a bad word to me about anyone in the family. I knew I had made her think, and I believe it made a great deal of difference to the family relationships from then on. If only I had been able to muster up the courage to speak my mind earlier.

My romance blossomed with the much-appreciated assistance of Royal Mail. John wrote regularly, and I spent hours writing to him every day. It helped enormously to pass the time. I lived for his letters which were quite romantic but always began with very detailed weather reports.

I think his obsession with the weather came about because of his tendency to be sea-sick. A naval career seemed to be a strange choice for someone who, as a child, had felt nauseous on a swing, but unfortunately for him, he had realized too late.

He tells the story of how proud he felt as he stood on the bridge of his first ship, in his brand-new uniform, sailing down the Manchester Ship Canal, and how he vomited immediately the ship went out into the rough water of Liverpool Bay. He recognized that he had chosen the wrong profession. His dubious claim to fame is that he has thrown up on every ocean in the world.

It was some years later that he admitted why he had chosen a naval career. It was not the call of the sea. An older school associate had spoken to him about his experiences as a radio officer in the Merchant Navy, and it had had instant appeal. That, he thought, sounded like a cushy number, and when the friend went on to describe his experiences sailing through the tropics with a permanent tan, meeting dusky young maidens in seedy bordellos, living a life of debauchery while getting paid, John was ready to board his first ship at the age of seventeen.

His father, not surprisingly, had other ideas, insisting that John complete grammar school before attending a naval college so that he could become "an officer and a gentleman." Before he could protest, he was shipped off to the School of Navigation at Warsash where he experienced the most gruelling years of his life.

John's father was greatly disturbed when he later learned of Lady Astor's opinion of merchant seamen. To her, they were anything but gentlemen. She called them "the scum of the earth," and said that they should not even be paid because they travelled around the world and received free food and board. She felt strongly that they should wear black arm bands to identify themselves.

Apparently, her daughter had become infected with a social disease following her liaison with one of them. It clearly devastated Lady Astor, as rumour has it that following the embarrassing infection, she put up a sign on her property which stated,

"No dogs or merchant seamen."

Once I had been privy to some of John's sea-going stories, I began to believe that Lady Astor was right. On his first voyage as an officer, he reported losing two crew members by the end of the second day—one with a venereal disease and one with a broken leg acquired in a drunken brawl—not unusual occurrences as it turned out.

I missed John, but I gradually adjusted to the idea of seeing him for only three weeks out of every six months. I had got to know his parents well enough that they often invited me to spend the weekend with them in Henley. Molly loved to be around people and was a great entertainer. A short, unsophisticated Welsh guest was preferable to no guest at all.

In their house, they ate lasagne and curry which to we simple Welsh people seemed quite exotic in those days. Nowadays, there is an Indian restaurant on every corner in every town and the Brits seem to eat nothing much other than take-out curry. Its popularity has even overtaken good old fish and chips.

Molly had resigned herself to her son choosing a short, unsophisticated girlfriend, and as long as we avoided mentioning Wales, all was well. Sue was dating a rather handsome French boy who she had met in France while studying hard for A-Levels. The French were looked upon somewhat more favourably by Molly.

In March, John came to Wales for a visit, and now that he had become an experienced redecorator, he volunteered to paint the outhouse for my mother. We had long since graduated from the refillable bucket to a posh chemical Elsen. He was fascinated by the fact that whenever he sat on the seat, the whole toilet descended a little closer to the floor because the bottom was starting to rust out. On his return to Henley, I am sure that the other members of the family were delighted that he had further material to enhance their usual conversations.

His decorating work was temporarily interrupted by

a sudden storm—it was all hands on deck. We had to drop everything and rush out to the fields to rake up the hay and cover it before it was ruined. I think he was stunned at how primitive life still seemed in parts of rural Wales in the early sixties.

On this occasion, Mr. Robinson kept a low profile, but my mother kept John entertained with stories of her experiences with ghosts. She told him that while she was having her hair done at the home of the local hairdresser, they both witnessed an old lady clad in Victorian dress passing the window. On investigation, the woman had disappeared into thin air. My mother also spoke of nightly, indeterminate footsteps on the gravel path leading up to the back door which caused the dog to bark frantically in response.

Gaining encouragement from John's obvious fascination, my mother then showed us an article from the local paper about a phantom dog that had been seen roaming around Tregare. She herself had seen a strange dog that looked more like a wolf crossing the road in front of her, just before Christmas.

"I wouldn't swear that it wasn't the actual phantom dog," she said, and then went on to tell us that friends of Haydn had seen a vision of Christ near Abergavenny on Christmas Eve.

I was convinced that these stories were figments of my mother's imagination, but John was a believer and consequently went to bed with one eye open.

Shortly before her death, my mother wrote to say,

"Well, I have finally seen the ghost."

Of course, we assumed it would have been "Ol' Robinson," but no, she described the ghost as a little wizened old lady dressed in a greying nightdress who approached her chair and protectively tucked a blanket around her legs. Her husband and the dog, we were told, witnessed it too. I was still sceptical, but when my mother became seriously ill, immediately after that visitation, and passed away the following year, I began to doubt my own scepticism.

As the British parliament adjourned for the summer recess in the summer of 1965, Pathé News showed clips of the Prime Minister, Harold Wilson, flying off to his summer house in the Scilly Isles and Edward Heath, the new leader of the Conservative Party, relaxing at his Mediterranean villa.

Not to be upstaged, John and I decided to head for exotic climes. We found an advertisement in *The Sunday Times* for Villa Party Holidays with the enticement of travelling by minibus for a bargain price. Young people in those days were regularly going overland to Marrakech, so we thought it would be a good adventure to go overland to Spain.

When we turned up at Charing Cross station, the designated meeting place, we were looking for a gleaming minibus with "Villa Party Tours" emblazoned along the side. We only noticed an old Bedford panelled van, with no side windows and the exhaust system held in position with baling wire, parked in a corner with two long haired hippies leaning against it, smoking.

A group of young women were gathering around it, and then we saw the two hippies beginning to pile the women's luggage on the roof. Could this be our minibus which was going to attempt to take us all the way to the Costa Brava? Yes, it could—twelve of us—eleven women and John. Well, *one* of us could anticipate having a good time; he knew that he was going to be the centre of attention.

The journey was horrendous; cramped together, on bench seats, we were driven to Dover, crossed the English Channel and travelled, at breakneck speed, through France into Spain in twenty-four hours. One of the passengers was so convinced that we would crash that she spent the whole journey lying on the floor in a foetal position, praying and crossing herself. Another girl,

Jane, had booked the trip in an attempt to recover from the recent loss of her boyfriend in a car crash and must have thought that she would be joining him imminently. She was a geography lecturer who gave a running commentary on all the geographical and geological features that we were racing by—that we could have seen if the van had had windows.

The drivers developed a very skilful driving rota. When one fell asleep and drove off the road, the other would be jolted awake and take over until the same thing happened to him. They were musicians who were practising for a gig and repeatedly sang the Beatles' hit, "It's Been a Hard Day's Night," and The Hollies "I'm Alive." Were they trying to tell us something?

At one point, the baler twine broke, and the muffler crashed onto the road, waking all the dogs in the town that we were passing through in the dead of night. We continued without it. It was the sort of journey that one would only choose to do once in a lifetime, but we were all sick at the thought of having to repeat it in just two more weeks.

As we crossed the border, a huge sign welcomed us—Bienvenidos a Espana!—but within seconds, a band of thugs appeared from nowhere and began beating up the minibus and spitting on the license plates— Bienvenidos indeed! Britain was desperately trying to cling onto one of the last vestiges of its once mighty empire, Gibraltar, and tensions between the countries were at an all-time high.

Well, how is Romeo going to extricate us from this plight? I wondered, but before he had a chance to demonstrate his chivalry, the driver put his foot down hard, and we sped onwards towards the coast leaving the protesters screaming obscenities in both English and Spanish behind us.

As we drew into Estartit, on the Costa Brava, the smell of Ambre Solaire mingling with fish and chips, "just like mother used to make," filled our nostrils. The Brits had already begun to ruin any authenticity on the Spanish coast, and Wimpy was already building developments as if there was no tomorrow. It would get much worse in the future.

Hordes of rowdy Brits were coming in on charter flights to drink themselves silly and engage in brawls on the streets.

It was a particularly social holiday. With my inability to consume much liquor, I became very ill on one occasion, after being handed a mixed drink. Going to the window for air, I threw open the shutters, knocking pots of geraniums three storeys down to the street below. Only moments later, I was squatting amongst the broken pots and upturned geraniums holding my head, convinced that I was going to die. John became very concerned about the hereditary propensity to alcoholism and, after tucking me into bed, went off to the disco to be consoled by Jane, the geography lecturer.

Feeling wretched, I trailed along to the beach with the others the following day. John willingly dug holes in the sand, so that I could vomit into them, and then he covered them up. I knew then, that this was a man who was well worth hanging on to. He was his father's son—a chip off the old block.

In September, I decided to leave Bristol with its sad memories for ever. I moved to Amersham, Buckinghamshire which was close to Henley and at the end of the Metropolitan line into London. I began teaching at St. Mary's Church of England School in Old Amersham.

At the same time, Andrew decided to move to Oxford, only a short distance from Amersham, to take his Masters' Degree. Anne had just transferred from London to teach in Bristol, so one can be forgiven for thinking that this was more than just a coincidence.

I made some very good friends at St. Mary's. Sheila Eldridge was teaching the reception class. She was a fresh-faced girl with a lovely smile, a great sense of humour and a heart of gold. She was newly married to David, a Gray's Inn lawyer, who was charming, and very fond of telling shaggy-dog stories. They recognized how lost and lonely I was in John's absence and took me under their wing. I was invited for Sunday lunches. Sheila was an excellent cook.

On our frequent trips to England, we have always made a beeline to their home, where they have continued to entertain us royally. Sheila has Parkinson's disease and following a fall has been almost completely paralyzed and confined to care. When we last saw her in 2012, she still had that beautiful smile and had not lost her sense of humour. Nor had David lost his penchant for long-winded jokes.

Jill, who is the only person who cannot be given her real name in this story, was single and living with her parents in a nearby town. Frequently, I spent the weekends at her home with her parents. Her father had retired from some high-ranking position in the army and was intimidatingly upper-class.

Jill's mother always asked a lot of questions and one day when she enquired,

"Was your father killed in the war?" I thought it was easier to lie and say yes, rather than try to explain that he was a raging alcoholic who was probably, at that moment, lying in a gutter somewhere in the east end of London. It was an insignificant lie, but I still feel uncomfortable about having told an untruth. In reality, I was still too embarrassed, even at the age of 23, to tell people that my parents were divorced.

Every week, Jill and I went to Oxford for the evening. While I hung out at Andrew's flat which he shared with his brother, Simon, or took in a play or a film, Jill went to visit her beau.

The following spring, while we were sitting on the living room floor at Jill's, she whispered out of her parents' earshot,

"I am going to need your help this week. I need you to lie for me."

I could not imagine what she was about to say, but if I had not been sitting, I would have fallen over when she continued,

"I need to have an abortion."

She said it as one would say, "I need to take a bath." I was quite stunned by her casual reference to something I considered to be so serious. I had never heard of anyone having an abortion. Fortunately, she had a relative who was a doctor in whom she could confide. She had made him swear never to tell her parents.

The following day, she went off to a clinic in London to undergo the procedure. The next day, she was back, facing her class, looking pale and drawn. She swore me to secrecy, and I have honoured her wish. What I did not consider is how emotionally traumatized she must have been by the experience, and what little comfort I was to her in that regard.

The subject was never broached again. The boyfriend was of another culture—Middle Eastern—a Muslim. John's mother's racial prejudice paled by comparison to that of Jill's parents'. Without question, they would have disowned her.

In July of 1966, John was due home from South America, but the dockworkers were on strike in England when his ship arrived off the shores of England, and it was not able to dock—so near and yet so far. He sent a telegram telling me to go to Hull, hardly the most romantic city in England, where his ship would dock once the strike was over. I had not seen him for five months. I booked into a hotel and waited. Eventually, by some means, he was able to get ashore that evening.

We had never discussed marriage, but the next morning, as we were ambling down the street, he said casually,

"Well, I suppose we should go and choose you a ring." John, ever the true romantic! It was quite unexpected, and I was overjoyed. We went to Samuels the jewellers, and I chose a diamond and sapphire ring which cost the princely sum of £25—the equivalent of $65. It will always be one of my most prized possessions. We planned the wedding for the following March.

His parents sounded very pleased when we phoned to tell them the news. Whether they really were is debatable. We could not contact my family, even if I had felt they would care. The only way to get a message to my mother would have been through the Bradleys, and it would have been somewhat insensitive to expect Tony to go running across the fields to deliver the joyful news of my engagement.

John then enjoyed an extended leave in England while taking his First Mate's Certificate and, for financial reasons, lived with his parents and travelled up to London every day. I went over to Henley most weekends to spend time with him and his irresponsible pals at the Rainbow.

In November, as the wedding day was approaching, John began to get cold feet. He was only 23 and felt that he was much too young to get married. He would be the first of his school friends to take the plunge.

One night, he came over to Amersham where I was then living over a dress shop with my roommate, Michelle. He told me he couldn't go through with the wedding. I was devastated. My reaction was rather more violent than it had been the first time around. We had a blazing row during which I threw the ring behind the bedroom chest where it remained for several weeks.

How could this be happening to me again? How could one person experience so much unhappiness in love? I began to have that childhood recurring dream all over again. I realized that my interpretation had been correct—my life was destined to continue on a shaky path. I would never ever find true happiness.

I wrote a long letter telling him that I never wanted to see him again which we both knew was anything but the truth, and we didn't see each other for about three weeks, during which time I was so distraught and missed him so much that I rescinded my threat, and, together, we fished the ring out from behind the chest the day before he went back to sea on a passenger ship—the Southern Cross—to Australia and New Zealand.

We arranged to get married at Harpsden, a little church not far from Henley. This pleased John's mum enormously, as she loved to organize events, and this gave her full rein.

Choosing Harpsden church was more complicated than I had anticipated. The vicar was a stickler for rules and I was not allowed to get married in his church unless I lived in the village. I moved in with friends of John's parents.

He also insisted on me attending the church and being interviewed by him. I thought it would be appropriate to take John's mother along for the interview. What a mistake! He asked me if we had been perfectly frank with each other about the physical side of marriage and discussed it sensibly. With my mother-in-law sitting beside me, I could hardly tell the vicar that this was a case of shutting the barn door after the horse had bolted.

He then went on to discuss "sexual positions" and asked me how much I had read on the subject. I didn't think he would approve of *The Perfumed Garden* so I remained silent. Believing, therefore, that I was sorely in need of education, he then loaned me a copy of *The Marriage Art*.

That afternoon, John's mother read it from cover to cover and then insisted that his father read it as well. They had been married for 28 years by then which leaves one to speculate on how much the book spiced up their sex life.

The night before the wedding, John, Sue and I were sitting around the dining room table with his mum discussing arrangements, when she suddenly burst into floods of tears and shocked us by telling us that she was illegitimate. It turned out that she had taken the name of a man who her mother eventually married, but her real name was not the one she had used all her life. For some reason, she thought that this might be revealed during the signing of the register the following day.

I felt such empathy for her. I could well imagine the anguish she had suffered with that on her mind for so many years. We completely understood why she had tried so hard to ensure that there would be no more illegitimate children in the family. She was also very concerned about how we would take the news of her mother's past life.

She didn't need to worry. For me, the news put the Dudley family on a similar footing to mine. It was good to know their closet had a few skeletons rattling around inside it. John and Sue were highly amused. They couldn't get over the fact that their sweet, quiet, old grandma had been what John called "a goer," in her time. We didn't know to what extent she had been "a goer" until, years later, we discovered that Molly also had an illegitimate sister.

Molly had died by the time that news surfaced. She would have been so thrilled to learn that she had a sibling, but she was denied that knowledge by relatives who, for appearances sake, decided to keep the "scandal" under wraps.

Next time I went to Wales, I told the family that if I had sisters or brothers of whom I had not been made aware, they had better confess immediately. Up until now, none have materialized, but I never give up hope.

My mind, however, kept dwelling on a strange incident involving my mother when I was a child. On my way home from Tregare school, I became aware of a commotion in the woods above the house. I could see my grandmother and Aunt Maisie leaning over my mother who was screaming hysterically and moaning as if in great pain. Not wishing them to be aware that I had seen anything, I scurried on home. I can't remember what happened in the interim, but my mother was nowhere to be seen, and the hushed whispers and knowing looks continued between all other members of the family throughout the evening. It struck me as strange that no doctor had been called. The doctor was always summoned to the house for any illness, however slight.

That night, when I went upstairs, my mother was already in bed sobbing and shivering uncontrollably. I didn't ask what was wrong, and she didn't volunteer anything, which was to be expected, but I was distraught to see her suffering and to be so completely shut out of the situation.

I have never asked anyone about that incident, and even if I had summoned up the courage, I have no doubt that my question would have been met with a stony silence. Being forced to spend a lifetime wondering what was the cause of my mother's distress that was such that it could not be discussed openly, I have been left to draw my own conclusions. On hearing John's mother's confession on the eve of our marriage, I began to wonder if perhaps the skeleton of my sibling is buried in the earth in the woods above Oakdale, or if he or she is living a secret life somewhere in Wales.

Our wedding took place on Easter Monday, March 27th—for income tax purposes—not, as it turned out, for the weather. It snowed. It was a very simple wedding completely without fanfare—not at all what John's mother wanted. She was annoyed that she could not persuade John to wear morning dress or his naval uniform. In any case, either outfit may have looked a bit too posh for my dress that had cost me £10 to make. John was not into posh. In every way, he is admirably devoid of affectation.

My husband-to-be had been the one with cold feet, but, on the day of our wedding, he was as cool as a cucumber while I was rigid with fear. I walked down the aisle like one in a medically induced coma. I remember nothing at all about the ceremony apart from Aunt Blodwen crying loudly throughout the proceedings, causing everyone to look in her direction which was, of course, her intention.

To add a little Welsh flavour, the hymns included "Cwm Rhondda"—Guide Me O Thou Great Redeemer.

Has anyone ever thought how inappropriate that hymn is for a wedding? "Death of Death and Hell's Destruction, Land me Safe on Canaan's Side?"—hardly an optimistic message for newlyweds.

The Welsh sat on one side of the aisle and the English on the other and ne'er the twain did meet. The singing was not exactly up to choir standard, and there were many snide comments by the English, afterwards, about the reputation of the Welsh as singers.

Our wedding day—left to right—cousin Andrea, John's parents, Will, the bride and groom, my mother, Uncle Philip, cousin Andrew and Sue—John's sister

The cool groom with his equally cool best man, William—Will

Following the ceremony, we gathered outside for the photographs, I still completely numb, but trying to smile with my lips stuck firmly to my teeth. I was vaguely aware of John and William, our best man, exchanging humorous quips and Aunt Blodwen still blubbering away in the churchyard, standing as far away from the rest of the Jones clan as she could, to avoid any association. She and Uncle Philip, the educated ones, had driven up to Henley together, while the rest of the Welsh contingent—the poor and huddled masses—had hired a bus for the occasion.

The whole event must have been very hard on my mother who was always out of her depth amongst strangers and away from home. My grandmother had refused to come to the wedding, but that was nothing unusual. She had not attended the weddings of any of her daughters.

At the reception, cousin Philip, who was not more than thirteen years old, got straight into the wine and was asleep within the hour, passed out cold on a chair. I heard, later, that on the way home, the bus had to stop several times for other members of the family to vomit on the side of the motorway. The Dudley branch of the family had plenty to talk about for years.

Following the reception, at which John gave a short but hilarious speech, referring to me as "the bird in white," we left on our honeymoon. It was the custom in England, at the time, for the bride and groom to "go away." What a ridiculous custom! We wanted to stay to enjoy the party.

Everyone was there to see us off. We hugged John's parents, and I hugged my mother for the first time in my adult life. It would have looked a little odd to hug John's mother but not my own. She was so shocked, she recoiled in horror.

Our honeymoon plans were set for walking the coves and beaches of Cornwall, breathing in the fresh, salty air tinged with the smell of seaweed, listening to the sound of surf pounding on the rocks. Alas! That was not to be.

On the eighteenth of March, the giant super tanker, Torrey Canyon, en-route to Milford Haven from Kuwait, took a shortcut between the Scilly Isles and the Cornish coast, hitting Pollard's Rock, spilling 32 million gallons of crude oil and contaminating 120 miles of the Cornish coastline.

We chose the Peak District instead, forgetting that the weather wasn't exactly spring-like at those latitudes.

We were very formally dressed—I in a new, white spring coat and John in his fancy corduroy jacket along with a crisp white shirt and a silk tie. He had not, however, true to English custom, forgotten his trusty Pac-a-Mac, in case of rain. What luck!

On the first night, we broke the journey at Bladon, the village where Winston Churchill had been buried at St. Martin's Church two years earlier. John had an excruciating headache, something from which he didn't normally suffer, so, although we had ordered a special dinner to mark the occasion, he was unable to eat a thing.

This was not the only setback. Our hotel was on the main Oxford road, and our room had been freshly painted, so we were faced with the choice of either being asphyxiated together on the first night of our marriage or being kept awake by the noise of traffic roaring past. I think we chose the latter option, although, at that point, John would possibly have preferred the first. I remember that my flimsy, sexy negligee that I had spent many hours sewing was for naught.

In Derbyshire, the rain never materialized, but the snow did, along with biting winds. We were not equipped for Arctic travel. The photographs in the album show us smiling stoically and looking as if we were having a wonderful time, but, in truth, we couldn't wait to return to Henley.

We called John's parents who were more than a little surprised when we asked if we could come home early. On the way south we stopped for a snack on the motorway to hear the recorded voice of Engelbert Humperdinck belting out "Release Me." Things had not got off to an illustrious start.

When we arrived home, John's mum had rearranged the beds so that we could have a double bed. I knew she still felt uncomfortable with the idea of us sleeping together under her roof.

MEMOIR OF "A SLOPPY, SPINELESS, CREATURE"

CHAPTER SEVENTEEN

"I learned very quickly that when you emigrate, you lose the crutches that have been your support; you must begin from zero, because the past is erased with a single stroke and no one cares where you're from or what you did before."
Isabel Allende

I left Amersham at the end of the spring term and got a temporary job in a primary school in Henley. Free Activity had not reached Henley yet, so I devised my own strategy towards individual learning. I think they call that I. E. P. now—Individualized Educational Plan—which sounds so completely innovative.

John had decided that he wanted to live in Canada, and I was in love, so I said that I would accompany him anywhere in the world. He could not wait to leave England. He was anxious to get away from the English class system and the inherited wealth that went with it, even though his life's experience had been nothing quite like mine.

His father was well educated and had a white-collar job. He had been brought up in a loving home in a close-knit family. Still, there were several aunts and uncles on Molly's side who had become successful entrepreneurs and wealthy businessmen who felt they were too superior to associate with a sister who had given birth to two illegitimate children. Molly and her family, therefore, were considered to be inferior to them and were shunned.

Despite my earlier experiences, I would never have left England if John had not wanted to go. He had suggested we go before we were married. It was a good try, but I did not fall for it.

He had left the navy much against my wishes and those of his parents. We all felt that he should take his

Master's Certificate. I was quite prepared to put up with the naval widow's life for another couple of years until he had acquired enough sea time, but he had heard of a job in Vancouver, through former colleagues, that did not require a Master's qualification, and he was determined to go. I don't think he ever lived to regret his decision, but qualifications, titles and status were very important to his parents.

While we were waiting to emigrate, until my term ended in July, we lived with my in-laws. That turned out to be a good move as, initially, they had been dreading us leaving, but after we had lived under the same roof for three months, they could not wait to see the back of us.

We spent a lot of Saturday evenings at the Rainbow, and we would both be feeling rather queasy on Sundays. When lunch was put on the table, nausea often caused us to push it aside. It was very unfair to his mother.

John's father also brought us tea in bed to get us up in the morning. We were very reluctant risers. The day we fell back to sleep and tipped the tea all over the bed, his father, who would, formerly, never have said a harsh word to anyone, berated us with,

"You have now sunk as low as you can go."

We heard from our friends, who had been told by their parents, that Molly and Harold couldn't wait for us to leave, but to their credit, they gritted their teeth and managed to keep the peace.

ROSE DUDLEY

Grey's Primary School in Henley—my class of 38 students

I was teaching a class of 38 seven-year-olds at Grey's Primary School and came home for lunch every day. John started a job with a building company to fill in the time, but by the middle of the first day, he had become unemployed. Returning for lunch, I found him with a good book, sunbathing in the garden. The next week, he started another job with a construction company and managed to stick that out for a whole day and a half before the manager suggested he find something less taxing. He had been filling a wheelbarrow with rocks and trying to wheel it across a narrow board. The wheelbarrow kept slipping off and refilling the hole as fast as the others were digging it out. John had demonstrated that he was not suited for heavy labour. So, on day two of that job, I found him back in the garden relaxing in his lawn chair again. What had I let myself in for? It was a very warm, sunny summer, and he was preserving his lovely tan while I was slogging it out in a hot classroom.

The following week, he acquired another job delivering pink paraffin to homes around Henley. The manager did not know the area very well so was not aware that John could complete his route in three hours, after which he could, once more, take up his position on his lawn chair. One of his customers happened to be Lee Radziwell—sister of Jackie Kennedy. That became his second claim to fame, but not fortune as she never paid her bills.

He managed to keep that job until the week before we left for Canada. After lunch, every day, he delivered me back to school. Not wanting my colleagues and the parents to know I had married the local paraffin man, I insisted he drop me off around the corner from the school entrance. This was Henley-on-Thames after all!

On several weekends, we went to Sussex where Tom had now graduated to ministering to cows, sheep and horses. We had visited him and Margaret on several occasions before we were married, but I was always a little sensitive about Margaret's younger sister, who was only sixteen at the time, knowing that we were sleeping in the same bed before we were married at the tender ages of 23 and 24.

"What kind of example are we setting?" I had asked—naively, as it turned out. Only a year later, Margaret's sister produced a baby.

Ten weeks after our marriage, I began to experience some rather tell-tale symptoms. I decided I would have to see a doctor. We didn't dare tell anyone else. The doctor confirmed that I was almost six weeks pregnant. This is not what we had intended, and we felt rather irresponsible since we were moving to a new country in less than four weeks.

While the thought of marriage had made John

nervous, the idea of becoming a father scared him out of his wits. He was just 24 and, as you will have gathered from my story, not the most responsible individual at that stage of his life. When I returned from the doctor, he was sitting in the bathtub, hoping against hope that it was all a big mistake. It wasn't.

He was afraid to tell his mother. He did not know what her reaction would be. I was the one who went to deliver the news, while he took the longest bath of his life.

Of course, he didn't need to worry. As I would find out, from my own experience later, the most exciting news for a middle-aged woman is to hear that she is about to become a grandmother.

Molly spent most of the evening on the phone to her friends, and the very next morning, she went off to Reading to buy baby clothing from Mothercare. We were back in favour.

Of course, as the time of our departure came nearer, we were feeling very apprehensive, not so much about leaving but how our families would be affected by our move.

We went to Wales to say goodbye to my family who had no idea if they would ever see us again. Once I became a mother myself, I realized how very hard it must have been for mine to see her only daughter departing for a place on the other side of the world.

She, my grandmother and Haydn came into the yard to see us off. My grandmother, clad, as usual, in apron and ventilated red Wellington boots, was all smiles and cracking jokes for John's benefit. He, like everyone who was not related to us, had always had such a hard time believing that she was such a tartar.

We did not hug because it was just not done in our family. We just stood there awkwardly, emotions sprung, not knowing quite how to leave, and then we just backed away slowly and got into the car, waving as we drove away. I felt an overwhelming sadness wash over me, but the tears would not fall.

The last week in Henley was very tense. We felt a little selfish going to the Rainbow to see our friends when we thought we should probably be spending time with John's parents. Molly had forgiven us for our inconsiderate behaviour, and as we wanted to go away on good terms we played our hands very carefully.

We had packed a big trunk mostly full of John's books and records. Many of our wedding presents had been in cash, so we did not have much in the way of worldly goods. Between us, we had £280—about $760 to our names.

Molly had made sure that her first grandchild would be the best dressed baby in Canada. In the week before our departure, she had almost bought out Mothercare, as well as all the baby wool from the Henley craft shop.

On the last night, our friends presented us with an antique, framed print of Henley which still holds pride of place in our home, and we bid them a fond farewell. They promised to write. Lee and her husband, Anthony Austin, always affectionately known as Tub, on again, off again lovers and next door neighbours, who married the following year, and Pete Jones, one of the San Sebastian trio, and his wife, Sally, are the only ones who have stuck faithfully to the bargain for almost 50 years. We have so much appreciated their regular Christmas notes with news of births, weddings and a new generation of Austins and Joneses.

William, always the poorest of communicators, has written to us only once, in response to our letter of condolence, when his young wife, Helen, dropped dead running in a race for charity, leaving him to care for four small children.

We managed to see him and Helen on one of our visits to England. At the time, we already had two daughters, and William, being in the medical profession, insisted that he knew of a fool-proof formula for conceiving a boy. We lost faith in the theory when he and Helen produced their third daughter just prior to us producing ours.

We caught up with William, again, in Scotland, in 2014, where we discovered that although he had been involved in cancer research for all his working life and had received the C.B E. for his contribution to medicine, he had continued to drink and smoke as heavily as he had done in his misspent youth.

John and I and our friends, Andrew and Ingrid, and David and Anne-Marie, were in Scotland to walk the West Highland Way—a distance of 92 miles, but Will was unable to walk around the block because of severe emphysema. It was sad to see our old friend in such poor physical shape, but what a wonderful time we had with him and Tub and Lee, reminiscing about the past.

The day of our departure to Canada dawned, and knowing how emotional Molly was at the best of times, we went to the airport in very low spirits. Neither of us had ever flown before, and we were about to travel halfway around the world. I was ten weeks pregnant.

At the airport, John's mother and Sue fed off each other's grief. It was a difficult parting. Since his mother was adamant that she would never fly, we believed that it would be a very long time before we would see each other, if ever. Sue told us that, returning home to our empty bedroom, his mother was inconsolable. The family felt that they had lost a part of themselves. They wandered from room to room, unable to settle into a life torn apart by loss.

It was the twenty-third of July 1967—the year that was coined the summer of love.

That was a reference to the pot-smoking teens who were grooving to the music of the Grateful Dead and similar bands that no longer had any appeal to prospective parents like us. We were leaving behind everyone we had known and everything that had been part of our lives for the last quarter of a century.

Soon, the plane took off, and I wept silently as I saw the green fields of England disappearing into the distance below me. We were on our way to Vancouver, British Columbia. I was filled with apprehension, not only about flying, but about what the future held in an unknown land.

The plane touched down first in Winnipeg where it had to refuel. Our next stop was Calgary where an enormous sign greeting us at the airport read,

"Howdy Pardner?"

Through the tiny airplane window, I peered out at the sign, the mostly deserted airport and the flat, barren expanse beyond.

"My God! He has brought me to the Wild West," I whispered under my breath.

I was seized with such a sense of doom.

EPILOGUE

"The people who affect your life and the downfalls you experience, they are the ones who create who you are. Even the bad experiences can be learned from. Those lessons are the hardest of all, but the most important."
Rashida Rowe

And what of those who were left behind—those who had influenced my life, one way and another, for better or worse, over the past twenty-five years?

My grandmother who, you will probably agree, had the greatest effect on my life, and, consequently, made my school life so difficult, continued to rule the roost at Oakdale, intimidating her family while charming outsiders, as was her way, until what normal people would have considered to be a happy event changed everything abruptly.

Everyone has heard about the eruption of Krakatoa in the Dutch East Indies in 1883, one of the deadliest and most destructive volcanic events in recorded history, but few know of a similar eruption at Oakdale, precipitated by the news that Uncle Philip, at the ripe old age of 51, had decided to finally brave it out and tell his mother that he was about to get married to Diana.

She literally went berserk. Only my mother and Haydn were left to witness the scene when Philip brought the good news from Gloucester to Tregare. How many mothers react to such news with threats to slit their throat under the stairs, end it all with a dose of rat poison or smash all the furniture and china to smithereens?

This, we learned, was exactly what happened for days on end, in the same way that the initial explosion of Krakatoa was followed intermittently by many more titanic eruptions.

Despite her bullying tactics, however, Philip, for once, held his ground. Diana had waited long enough and was probably, by then, issuing her own ultimatum. The marriage was going ahead, come what may.

My grandmother had managed to exert her power over her family for a lifetime. She was accustomed to winning. She wasn't about to readily accept any loss of control. Having exhausted all other blustering means of intimidation, she chose a desperate option. Impervious to reason, she packed her bags and left Oakdale, believing that this final act would prevent the marriage. It only served to put her in a losing position from which she could never back down—too stubborn and too proud to change course.

She moved in with Aunt Blodwen, to a depressing little maisonette in Cwmbran, New Town—one of those completely soulless places that had been constructed after the war—the kind of place that makes the happiest of people contemplate throwing themselves under a bus.

How my grandmother must have regretted her abrupt decision. In Cwmbran, she was a lost soul—bereft of a life—lonely and unhappy. Aunt Blodwen still worked full-time at the local mental hospital at Llanfrechfa, so my grandmother was left alone all day with little to do and not a living soul around with whom she could communicate.

Her hope, of course, was that the rest of the family would plead for her to come home—to say that the farm could not be run without her—but, alas, that did not happen. She had been defeated. The feisty character that she had been was no more. She had lived at Oakdale for 60 years, the only place in her adult life she had known. She would never return.

Initially, she took nothing with her that would harbour any painful memories of her old home, but as the years passed, she became conscious of the absence of "The Maiden's Prayer" and instructed Haydn to deliver it.

On his way to Cwmbran, a car coming in the

opposite direction in the narrow lane, drove him off the road, through a hedge and into a field full of astonished cows. "The Maiden's Prayer" was smashed to smithereens. Haydn burst into fits of hysterical laughter when it was revealed that it was fake—that the image was not painted on glass but was a cheap poster mounted under glass. He is laughing still, but, to me, it seemed like the ultimate metaphor for our lives.

Haydn and my mother picked up the pieces at Oakdale, until Aunt Phyllis and her family could move in with Haydn to continue running the farm.

I saw my grandmother only twice after the move— the last time when she was 83 years old. I was unnerved by the change in her. How could this frail, meek, old lady in dark glasses, with papery thin, sallow skin and straight white hair be the same person who had terrorized two generations?—the fight gone out of her—the volcano spent.

Four generations,—taken on an earlier trip in 1969—my grandmother at 81—still a Tony home permanent devotee, at that stage

She spoke so quietly and kindly and seemed genuinely pleased to see me and my two children, Helen and baby Alison, but there was the same awkwardness in the room, as we endeavoured to think of things to say to each other—to find common ground.

Aunt Blodwen, now even more rotund, sat rocking back and forth in her chair, rubbing her red, leather bedroom slippers together, the squeaking thunderous in the bloated silence, while repeatedly pushing up her glasses to better survey the scene. Her equally obese dog, Cindy, rolled around on the hair-covered carpet in front of us.

Breaking the silence, my grandmother struggled up from her hard-backed chair in the corner and hobbled, with the aid of a stick, across to the fireplace. Winding up a music box that I had brought back from Switzerland on my hitch-hiking trip with my college friends, many years earlier, she whispered,

"I've played this every single day since you've been gone, our Rosie."

Hearing the mournful sounds of Edelweiss issuing forth from that carved box, I was overcome with emotion. Removing myself to the garden, with Alison in my arms, the floodgates opened, and I cried the oceans of tears that had been welling up for all the years past. I sobbed for what might have been. But, my tears were restorative, like a dam that bursts, with an initial deluge, and eventually becomes that little stream reverting to nature's intended course.

I never saw her again. She died only two years later. I weep to think of her spending her last years in that dreary place where she didn't belong and becoming a person to whom we could no longer relate—who we could barely recognize.

Haydn continued to live at Oakdale, reunited with his mother and stepfather. He lives there still with my Uncle Bill who, by his own judgement has been on the verge of death for the last ten years but will likely be receiving a telegram from the Queen shortly.

Aunt Phyllis died far too young, at the age of 70, from an undiagnosed respiratory ailment. I miss her more than I can say.

Uncle Ginge, Maisie's husband, had died of throat cancer some years earlier, caused, no doubt, by his heavy drinking and smoking. Even on his death, my grandmother couldn't bring herself to utter a good word about him:

"Good riddance, I say. We are all better off without the likes of that bloody rotter," was her parting shot as she marched out of the churchyard, following the burial.

Maisie did alright for herself. She inherited the harmonium, minus the cacti, and had it restored to its Victorian glory. She bought a large Edwardian house in Monmouth and divided it into many flats. Her "weak heart" continued to tick until she was well into her eighties and would be ticking still if a fall had not resulted in a broken hip for which she stubbornly refused treatment.

Aunt Blodwen lived on in her cheerless maisonette in Cwmbran until she, too, had a fall for which she was unable to call for help, precipitating an awful, lonely death at 85. I wish I had thanked her for her kindness and generosity towards me, while I still had the chance.

Molly conquered her fear of flying through necessity. She and Harold visited us many times. We got along well, in later years. She hadn't really liked me at first, but it didn't matter. I knew that her dislike had nothing to do with the fact that I was short or unsophisticated or even Welsh. She would not have liked anyone who married her "wonderful son." I had replaced her in his love. She was not unlike any other mothers of "wonderful sons."

Harold and Molly loved Canada but always told us that they could never imagine living where we had chosen to live—the tiny village of Lions Bay—the back of beyond in their view.

On one of their visits, "the wonderful son" did something quite out of character; he thought it would be a great idea to have a "boys" day out with his father. He took him to Blaine, in Washington State to see an adult movie—they were banned in Canada at that time.

On the way there, John's father asked,

"Will it be a bit salty?"

He had no idea what he was in for. It was a double feature: "Deep Throat," starring Linda Lovelace followed by "The Devil in Miss Jones"—no known relation.

On returning home, my father-in-law declared that he had been put off sex for life to which my mother-in-law murmured, "Thank God for that!"

John's parents both died far too young. Harold succumbed to lung cancer at 63; he had smoked all his life at a time when people didn't want to believe that smoking caused cancer. I often think about all those packages of St. Bruno Flake I bought for him on my many visits. Molly died of oesophageal cancer at 70—likely the result of inhaling second hand smoke for so many years. All her ancestors had lived well into their nineties so we had assumed that she would too. Her death was a huge loss to our family.

Lyn and Sue were married only two years after we emigrated, and Molly finally got the wedding she had not been able to orchestrate for John.

Sue and Lyn's wedding—July 1969

Molly finally got to see her "wonderful son" in morning dress.

They live in a beautiful part of England, close to the Seven Sisters in East Sussex—those stunning chalk cliffs that seem to feature in so many films.

All my teachers have long passed on. I remember them with mixed emotions. Mrs. Powell had always followed my progress with interest, and, on one of my visits to Wales, I took her out for tea and Welsh cakes in a Monmouth tea shop, to show her how grateful I was for her positive influence in my life. In her advancing years, she was still what my grandmother would have called a "floozy"—blond coiffed hair, manicured nails and bright red lipstick, but, to me, she was the teacher that all should wish to emulate.

Mrs. Powell—my first teacher—still "a floozy" in her fifties

The kindness and respect shown to students by the staff at Barrow Court did much to restore my faith in humanity and boost my feeling of self-worth. I remember them with enormous gratitude and affection.

In my advancing years, I reflect on those who were so hard on me. Did Miss Whatley's bitter words turn my anger into repudiation of her opinion? Did Miss MacDonald's words give me the determination to prove something? Recently, I was relating my humiliating school experiences to a well-grounded cycling friend, Joyce. Her carefully measured words surprised me:

"But you were so fortunate that they cared enough about you to give you that chance in life."

Was I disappointed in her response? Was I still looking for sympathy? Those words provided me with a new perspective. I knew they were wise words indeed and, deep down, I had known it for a long time.

I think profoundly about the life that Haydn has lived compared to mine. Although I have led a happy, successful life here in Canada, I wonder if I would have been as happy and contented as he appears to have been in Tregare—seemingly devoid of the hangups I suffered—if my life had not taken that drastic turn at age eleven? On the surface, he has always been so thoroughly at ease with his family and his simple life in the country. Would that have been so, if the shoe had been on the other foot—that he had been made to feel that the life into which he was born was not good enough?

On his only visit to Canada, we made every effort to show him the "good life" and, condescendingly, I realize now, thought how much it would broaden his horizons. While he loved his visit and talks about it to this day, he has never had the slightest desire to leave Tregare where he has lived so happily amongst his own people: —pottering around in his garden, raising bedding plants in his greenhouse to supply the neighbours, growing show-standard flowers and vegetables, rescuing battery chickens to live out humane lives on the farm, playing skittles while enjoying a beer at the pub with his few close working-class friends. To coin a phrase, "He's as happy as a pig in shit."

The "two little bastards"—now two old bastards—2016—at 74 and 78

I, on the other hand, fashioned Hazel's words into a truism. For years, I was in limbo, having turned against my family and all those with whom I had grown up, because I thought I no longer had anything in common with them. In other words—Hazel's words—I had been turned, against my will, into a snob.

I have not seen Hazel for many years. She married young and has since divorced as has my faithful old friend Tony. They still live in the Monmouth area, so it is not too late for me to look them up—to revisit our childhood years together—even to ask Tony to take me dancing for old-times' sake.

Uncle Philip and Aunt Marion are living into ripe old age. They have both meant so much to me throughout my life, and it is such a pleasure to visit them and see how fit and well they are; they are both still avid gardeners. Mentally, too, they are so alert; they have maintained a sense of humour and take a keen interest in world affairs. I have learned, as have her long-suffering children, that having an argument on any topic with Aunt Marion is not one that anyone is likely to win.

It might be time for me to tell my uncle and aunt how much I appreciate them—to break down some of those barriers, have the conversations that have never happened and ask all the questions that have never been answered. One of those would be to ask Uncle Philip why he has continued to conceal the details of his life from his family.

Uncle Philip, 98, and Aunt Marion, 91, with John. Diana in the foreground—2016

As far as anyone knew, he and Diana were living near Ross-on-Wye, but before Haydn retired from his job with the Welsh Water Board, he was called to a home in Monmouth to investigate the report of a leaking pipe. He was completely floored when Uncle Philip opened the front door. He had been living in Monmouth, just seven miles from the family home and only three miles from his sister's home for many years but had never disclosed his whereabouts to anyone. At the age of 97, could he still be feeling embarrassed about his family?

The original John—original in every sense of the word—moved to America. Perhaps he is one of the rare individuals who knew how to cope with the British class system. He seems to have continued to be of the "if you can't beat 'em, join 'em" persuasion. I know that he loves to return to England, in the hunting season, to hobnob with the gentry, and I'm sure he manages to carry it off magnificently, just as he always did. I admire him for it.

Tom and Margaret also left Britain and have recently celebrated their fiftieth wedding anniversary in Saskatoon, Canada. The promise of better employment opportunities with higher salaries certainly encouraged droves of young people to emigrate during the sixties and seventies. Many of our transplanted British friends came at that time. Some of them are still carrying hefty chips on their shoulders that they imported with them. It has taken a chainsaw for me to rid me of mine.

While Haydn and I have never openly discussed our true feelings about how we were affected by our grandmother, apart from laughing over her foibles, I know he would find my stories of her behaviour much too harsh. He would only remember the good times, while I have allowed them to become obscured, in my mind, by the hurt.

When my grandmother passed away in 1973, I did not go back to Wales for her funeral, but I heard that Haydn was the one who cried the most over her death. I was not the slightest bit surprised—forgiveness has always come so easily for him.

I went home to Wales often, when the children were young, so that they would have the opportunity to get to know their grandmother. I had never really thought much about how our departure to a land so far away might have affected my mother, but on our arrival on the first visit back to Wales, we were unnerved to find that our bed was still in the same state in which we had left it two years earlier—the same sheets still on it, the bedding thrown back and cobwebs forming across the headboard. She had not made any preparation for our arrival with a baby, and I realized then just what our leaving had done to her. She had sunk into a deep depression.

I believe she may have been suffering from depression for many years, which would account, in part, for her inability to communicate effectively. Why was I not able to recognize the symptoms? Why did I not ask her how she felt? Would things have been any different if I had? She had not had a very rewarding life. Her upbringing had been the cause of her making poor decisions as a young adult, so robbing her of the opportunity for a lasting, loving relationship.

On our return to England in 1970, John and I contacted my father. He was going through an alcohol-free period, managing to hold down a job in London, at the time. I did not inform my mother that I had made contact but, on learning that she was still living in the same house and had not remarried, he decided to go to see her.

She was very welcoming, and for a year or more after his first visit he travelled down to Wales every weekend. She wrote to tell me that they had been reunited, and I was delighted for her. I was twenty-six years old, but it was the first time that she had mentioned my father's name since the days of Anne Driver's dance programme, when I was three years old.

About a year after their happy reunion, she took my father to Newport to catch the train back to London, as she had done every Sunday evening. She never saw him or heard from him again. He had returned to a life of drinking. I was mortified that, indirectly, I had been the cause of further unhappiness in her life.

My father died in a Catholic refuge for alcoholics in London in 1985 at the age of 70. My grandmother had passed away by then, but I could almost hear that voice emanating from the grave:

"For a bloody rotter like 'im who 'ad pissed 'is life away with drink, fags and whores, 'e 'ad a good innin's. Nobody should feel sorry for that bugger."

Some years later, my mother applied for a job as a cook at a Butlin's holiday camp in Bognor Regis. How desperate she must have been for company, to do something so out of character—to go to work at a place where she would have been expected to dress in that red coat uniform and where the slogan was "A Little Bit of This and Quite a Lot of That."

How apropos was that slogan, as it turned out. After living alone for 30 years following her divorce from my alcoholic father, she met another alcoholic, Richard, with whom she lived until she died.

The year before her death, she brought him to Canada. Thinking that it would be the moral thing to do because of our children, she married him prior to coming.

She had never made us privy to the fact that he was an alcoholic, so when, on the first day of the visit, our very sociable neighbours, Flo and Harold, burst into the garden bearing a tray of exotic drinks, we were cognizant of the fact that my mother looked distressed, but we had no idea why—that Richard should not partake.

One drink was all that it took for us to understand the problem, so we immediately cleared the house of all liquor. In desperation, he began to steal bottles from the neighbours. After we had managed to sober him up, he was so embarrassed by his behaviour that he returned to Wales early, completely ruining the holiday for my mother.

Following his departure, she talked, constantly, about a new position she was being forced to take on her return to Wales. Tregare school had finally closed, so she was being transferred to a larger school where there would be a central kitchen with many cooks. She had been her own boss for so many years that she was very nervous about moving into such an unfamiliar situation. I thought about it, but I don't know what prevented me from telling her that she did not need to take the job. She had amassed a reasonable amount of superannuation and now had a husband, of sorts, who also had a pension. She could have easily retired. She could have moved to Canada to live with us. There were so many options.

My mother and Aunt Phyllis in the school kitchen two years before Tregare school closed

She had only been in the new position for a few weeks when she became seriously ill. Could stress have played a part in her illness? She was only 56 years old when a call came from Aunt Blodwen to tell me that my mother was in hospital and not expected to live. She had always been such a strong, healthy woman, so it was almost impossible for me to believe that she now lay dying in Cardiff Royal Infirmary.

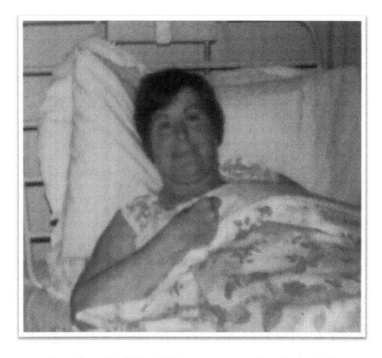

My mother in Cardiff Royal Infirmary just six months before her death

The family had already made the decision that she should not be told that she had terminal cancer. I argued that my sudden arrival on the scene would cause her to be somewhat suspicious, which, of course, it did. When I appeared at her bedside her first, almost angry, words were,

"What on earth are you doing here?"

I concocted a convincing story, and whether she believed me or not, she was so pleased to have me visiting her at the hospital every day for a few weeks that the subject never arose again.

She was undergoing radiation treatment which had considerably reduced her pain, so she was in good spirits but full of stories about the "poor woman" who was terminally ill in the next bed. I couldn't quite believe that a person of her intelligence did not suspect that she also had cancer, but if she did, I understood her well enough to know that she would not question me.

Misleading her about her prognosis made me feel very uncomfortable, but the family had made the decision and, who knows?—perhaps it was the right one. We spent three pleasant weeks together, although our conversation was, as usual, superficial and unemotional.

The day that I left her, I managed a cheerful parting and drove to Bargoed where my old friend, Mike Phillips, the grandson of the Reverend Phillips, was then living with his wife, Audrey, having recently returned from Canada. It was a dark and stormy night as I headed alone, along unfamiliar roads into the Welsh valleys, blinded by the rain, my tears and a mass of confusing road signs in both Welsh and English. I sensed that I would never see my mother again.

I have frequently laboured over the family's decision not to tell her the truth. Was it the right one for her or was it the one that made it easier for us?

Deprived of a last goodbye,
Your smile not sensing
The snowdrops will not bloom again for you.
No hugs, no kisses—it's not our way.
Bound by a family's lie
We back away
A contrived smile
Concealing the truth along with our grief.
Was it our judgement to make?
A gesture of love

Or the final abandonment?

Every person we meet in life, in some way has an influence on the person we become, but I reflect, also, on how I might have influenced the lives of others. I think of my family—how I shunned them, believing that I had been educated out of my class. I particularly think of my mother who was so anxious for me to have a good education but how, in the pursuit of it, I became someone to whom she could no longer relate. Between us there developed a chasm that became wider and deeper, with the passing years, that neither of us could find the strength or the will to cross.

Life is full of regrets. How many of us have uttered those words, "If only," time and time again? Ultimately, we are all products of our upbringing and, as such, we can regret deeply, but can we be blamed for our shortcomings? Haydn would say that that is the reason why we need to understand and forgive our grandmother.

I acknowledge that I am not the submissive, irresolute person I once was. I no longer think of myself as a spineless, amoebic low-life. Friends and acquaintances, hearing the title of my memoir, find it difficult to believe that I was once the tortured soul hidden amongst these pages.

"You?" they laugh, "That cannot be true—sloppy?—spineless?—never!

Over time, I suppose I have developed the backbone to seek out comforts and successes to set against the early blows. Maybe old Friedrich Nietzsche got it right, after all:

"That which does not kill us makes us stronger."

MEMOIR OF "A SLOPPY, SPINELESS, CREATURE"

ACKNOWLEDGEMENTS

My thanks are expressed to Patrick Hill, author of *Where do you go at Night?* and *Cruise the Alaska Coast*, whose dedication to his writing was my inspiration, to Reagan D'Andrade, my first and only writing teacher, who provided such a safe and warm environment for me and my classmates to take those first faltering steps into writing and made us all believe that we had the ability to succeed, to: Patrick and Heather Hill, Rose and Rob Dickinson and Jytte and Zoltan Kiss who enthusiastically followed my daily progress and urged me on as I tapped away at the computer under the palm trees of Huatulco, to Robin Spano of Lions Bay, herself a published author, who, having read my first three chapters, convinced me that my story was worth telling, to: Rod Baker, author of *Constant Traveller*—a memoir, I *Need my Yacht by Friday* and *Um Where is Belize?*—A Journey Into the Unknown, and Karen Dodd, author of *Deadly Switch*, who shared valuable information on the ups and downs of self-publishing, to my friend, Andrew Wray, who, with the patience of Job, assisted me in unfolding the mysteries of technology, to: my daughter, Helen, my son-in-law, Wyatt, and my granddaughter, Amanda, for unfailing technical support, to: my good friend and teaching partner, Diana Bedford, and her daughter, Holly, for their scrupulous proofreading, to my young friend, Clare Guinan of York, England, whose editing skill and constructive advice improved the original manuscript, to: Sally Stirrit who permitted me to use her fitting words describing the Barrow Court staff and her heartfelt poem of dedication to the warden, Dagmar Andersen, and Katherine MacPhee who allowed me to include her late mother's pertinent quote from *Picasso's Woman*, a memoir chronicling her illness, to: my family and friends who have tolerated my Welsh foibles with patience and humour, but most of all, to my husband, John, who makes me laugh every day and has taught me that the important thing in life is not where you come from, who you are or what you have, but what you give to others.

ABOUT THE AUTHOR

Rose Dudley grew up in South Wales and attended school in Monmouth.

Following her teacher training in Somerset, she taught in infants' schools in Bristol and Amersham, England, before emigrating to Canada with her husband, John, in 1967.

Since 1972, she and John have lived on the shores of Howe Sound, in the stunningly beautiful village of Lions Bay, British Columbia.

They have three married daughters and seven grandchildren.

Made in the USA
Columbia, SC
25 November 2017